The World of Bryan MacMahon

edited by Gabriel Fitzmaurice

D1334253

MERCIER PRESS

Mercier Press
Douglas Village, Cork
Email: books@mercierpress.ie
Website: www.mercierpress.ie

Trade enquiries to CMD Distribution
55A Spruce Avenue, Stillorgan Industrial Park
Blackrock, County Dublin
Tel: (01) 294 2560; Fax: (01) 294 2564
E-mail: cmd@columba.ie

ISBN 185635 467 9
10 9 8 7 6 5 4 3 2 1

A CIP record for this title is available
from the British Library

Front cover: photograph of Bryan MacMahon (1932) reproduced by kind
permission of Maurice McMahon.
Back cover: photograph of Peig Sayers reproduced by kind permission of
The Great Blasket Centre, Dunquin, Co. Kerry.

Mercier Press receives financial assistance from
the Arts Council/An Chomhairle Ealaíon

Printed and Bound by J. H. Haynes & Co. Ltd, Sparkford

CONTENTS

INTRODUCTION

In July 2003, in my capacity as director of Tarbert Education Centre in north Kerry, I organised a teachers' summer course based on the life and works of John B. Keane. This proved such a resounding success that (a) Mercier Press published a book of essays entitled *Come All Good Men and True: Essays from the John B. Keane Symposium* from the proceedings and (b) we were encouraged to hold a symposium on the world of Bryan MacMahon in July 2004. This, again, was a summer course for primary teachers and, with one eye on the inspectors in the Department of Education and Science (who could sanction or refuse the course), we came up with a title that would satisfy the department and, more importantly, would describe what we in Tarbert Education Centre hoped to achieve from the course. We called the course 'Literature in the Locality: the Writer and the Curriculum as Exemplified in the Writing and Teaching of Bryan MacMahon'.

Let us pause a moment to consider the title. It is not all about literary criticism; it is not all about local studies; it is not all about the curriculum for national schools; it is not all about Bryan MacMahon, teacher; it is not all about the history of education. Rather it is, as the title of this book suggests, about the world of Bryan MacMahon: Bryan MacMahon the story-man, the master, the balladmaker, the Gaeilgeoir and translator of Peig Sayers' autobiography; Bryan MacMahon the inheritor of the hedge schools of the nineteenth-century and a pioneer of education in the national schools in the new Irish state. It is about the world of Bryan MacMahon, the world he inherited, the world he inhabited, the world he helped to shape.

Bryan MacMahon lived all his life in his native Listowel.

He taught in the primary school where he had begun his education as a pupil; he taught generations of Listowel boys, among
them John B. Keane, in this school. He wrote out of that environment – 'Hero Town' he has called it, and if anybody could
make a hero town of a small country town in the south-west of
Ireland, MacMahon, with his knowledge of local character and
colour, could. He could write from his hero town because he
had a vision that could both report and imagine it. Throughout
his long life he could see the world through the eyes of a child
and bring that freshness, that vivacity, to the maturity of his
adult writing.

As a teacher he demonstrated that one need not be bogged
down and constricted in a small rural town, or village for that
matter. One could, indeed should, seek out the genius of the
place – the unusual, the bizarre, the estranged, as much as the
more orthodox heroes and heroines of one's society. He
famously stated that he wanted to take a small country town
and turn it into a centre of the imagination. And he succeeded
in his short-stories, his novels, his plays, his ballads, his translations and his memoirs. His test for authenticity was that a
piece of writing have one foot in the cow-dung. Bryan Mac-
Mahon's work is firmly rooted in the cow-dung, in the fertile
expression of his native place. He was a man who could meet
the world on his own terms in his native Listowel, the hero
town of his imagination.

In putting this book together, I hope that the reader will
enter the world of Bryan MacMahon and be nourished and
enlightened – and encouraged – by his commitment, his compassion, his vision. In *The World of Bryan MacMahon*, Mac-
Mahon stands for a whole generation of Irish men and women
whose vision of Ireland helped found the new state. This state

was not without its blemishes – poverty, mass emigration, clerical oppression, censorship – but those men and women survived to hand on the torch of their bright vision, their *aisling gheal*, to us, the leaders, the teachers, the parents, the children of the twenty-first century. It behoves us, keepers of the flame, to respect and refine that vision. If this book helps in any small way, our project will have been worthwhile.

Gabriel Fitzmaurice
Director, Tarbert Education Centre
October 2004

CHAPTER ONE

Bryan MacMahon – Údar agus Oide

Owen D. McMahon

In this article I would like to examine and reveal the main influences on and sources of inspiration of Bryan MacMahon in his life and in his twin roles of *údar agus oide* (writer and teacher). These are not my labels, they were chosen by himself prior to his death for his epitaph and in using these terms he left strict instructions that they were to describe his life work, no more, no less.

The influences I have identified could be summarised as the three Ps: period, place and people. I will endeavour to deal with these individually and use some quotations from his works and anecdotes, which he related to us, to illustrate the effect that place and people had on him as a writer and teacher.

Period
Bryan MacMahon began teaching shortly after the birth of the Irish Free State and immediately identified the importance of education and the opportunities it could afford to the ordinary people. All during this period the catch cry which was ringing in his head was the Thomas Davis quotation:

Educate that you may be free.

This ideal he transferred to his pupils (even in devious and simplified form), that in the Ireland of the future there would only be one aristocracy, not that of privilege, but that of ability. He realised that without a vision the people perished and that there was nowhere the children could move on the social ladder except upwards.

'A good teacher,' he once said, 'could leave the print of his teeth on a parish for three generations.' This he endeavoured to do by realising that each child had a gift, and that the encouragement of this gift was the proper goal of teaching. To him a great teacher was simply a great person teaching. From the quotation below from *The Master*, we can appreciate and identify what drove him all through his teaching career.

Now after a long period in servitude and even in squalor, when our state is only a few short years in existence, I feel I have the duty to pay back to Ireland in general, and to this village in particular some of the educational debt I already owe my country. I am I suppose in one sense, an idealist and that is why I am here. I believe that there are three hungers in Man, the hunger of the spirit, the hunger of the body and the hunger of the imagination and if Man is to exist in harmony with himself, then these three hungers must be in the balance. The hunger of the spirit, I shall deal with in Christian Doctrine class. The hunger of the body is appeased by the potatoes, ice cream, bread, apples and so on. The hunger of the imagination, concerns me deeply, and is appeased by poetry, affection, flowers, beauty of a landscape. For me a story is everything and everything is a story. Christ was a storyteller. I shall also reference the uniqueness of each one of you, chiefly by means of the imagination and a story. A people need an ideal, a holy grail, or else it will perish. Without a vision, the prophet of old has said, 'the people die'. I believe that every child has the right to be educated to the peak of his/her abilities. I also believe that each child is born with a gift. That gift, if is it not developed, is like a bell that is not rung.

MacMahon also imparted to his pupils the importance of being an avid reader and what a gift a good book was. If there is one factor common to all school subjects it is that of reading, the interpreting of ciphers, a process that constitutes a mystery for every child. The pupil must be lured to enter the mystery, to explore this magic cave, before he can unlock the secrets of the world about him. MacMahon identified reading as the most important activity of the school day. Given the gift of reading, the child can solve, from his own resources, many of the problems that confront him in life and also find it a source of almost unending pleasure. The greatest intellectual disadvantage that anyone can carry through life is the inability to read. From a facility in reading springs a love of writing with its embodiment of a person's creativity and also, with luck, an appreciation of such ancillary aesthetics as poetry and song:

> A book has a thousand roles, it can be comforter, informer, healer, enthuser, sedative, elucidator, disturber of the peace, priest, Satan, Messiah, physician of the mind and rabble rouser.

He would read to his pupils every day and tell them stories, particularly at the end of the school day, so that each pupil would leave the class with a sweet taste in their mouth and an appetite to return the following day, eager to learn and find out how the story ended. I am reminded of the story of one incident during an English reading lesson. The story contained the word 'rickshaw'. MacMahon enquired from the class if any boy knew the meaning of this word, but no pupil could answer. As an incentive, he in turn offered the prize of sixpence, one shilling, two shillings and half a crown to any boy who could give the meaning of this strange word. There were no takers. He closed the book in disappointment and ended the lesson. On his way home that evening, he met a neighbour, whose son, Thomas, was in his class and he recounted to her the events of the day, knowing full well that Thomas' mother would tell her son the meaning of the word. The following day he again opened the English reader and asked the same question of the class about the meaning of the word 'rickshaw'. He was met with a stony silence. Again he offered financial rewards, of sixpence, one shilling and two shillings but he did not receive any reply. Before offering the ultimate reward of half a crown, he walked the length of the classroom, put his hand on Thomas' shoulder and said: 'Here's a boy, whose mother told him the meaning of the work "rickshaw" last night, but hasn't he forgotten it already.' Poor Thomas, who had been waiting to pounce once the half crown was offered, was shattered to see the dream of instant riches snapped from his grasp.

The common cry of children, he always said, was 'Tell us a story!' and this he did all through his teaching life. A teacher was an actor, playing on the front lawns of the children's minds, who had to entertain, perform, educate, hold their attention, amuse and control the youthful audience for up to six hours a day. No wonder he was tired after a day's teaching, although he soon regained energy and enthusiasm after a cat nap in the afternoon!

Place

So many places influenced Bryan MacMahon that it is difficult to know where to start. He once said that he came from a town where everybody was a storyteller. Certainly such places as the marketplace, the forge, the harnessmakers' shops, the book-shop, the library, the mart, the town, the square, the street, the river and the school were all places which influenced him deeply all during his life.

The marketplace, which was directly behind the house where he was reared, was just one example of a place where MacMahon began to engage the people of town and country. What a wonderland the market proved to be, as he haunted the place in the impressionable years as he grew into adolescence. The place was occupied in one form or another almost every day of the week. Calf market, pig market, butter market, hay and straw market, vegetable market, all found it thronged with farmers and noisy with the shouting, arguing and the ballad-singing of men.

In greeting those he met he always used the traditional greeting of 'Conas tán tu?' (How are you?) In a lifetime, he assembled over forty different answers to this question in-cluding 'pulling the devil by the tail', 'living but not high', 'my day is sound when I'm over ground', 'keeping the best side out like the broken mug on the dresser', 'dodging the undertaker', 'battling bravely against bladder and bowel' and 'I'm too poor to paint and too poor to whitewash'. These he referred to as the 'Bank of Say' and each individual reply he treasured like a jewel. If he received a new reply his day was made. I think he would have enjoyed the reply I received to the same question recently when I met an old woman in a rural pub. I queried her: 'What way are you Minnie?' To which she replied: 'Yerra, what way would I be?' I continued: 'And what way is Jack, your hus-band?' She retorted: 'There is a devil a fear of my Jack, for he eats my pension and drinks his own.' (Had Jack discovered the secret of a happy life?)

And so he wandered from Bunyan's forge to Moss Scanlon's and Paddy Finunace's harnessmakers' shops to Dan Flavin's bookshop, attending at the University of Life. He established where he lived in terms of place as defined by market, river and community. However, these were only some of his coordinates and like it or not he had to ascertain or recognise where he stood in terms of wider place and elusive time. He simply had to find his bearings, where he stood in terms of time and also in the context of the story of his people.

His sense of place is most evident in his first novel, *The Children of the Rainbow* (which was based on the happenings of his youth and adolescence in the village of Cloone), and in his last novel, *Hero Town* (in which he records the epiphanies of the passing days in his beloved Listowel).

People/Community

In writing, it became apparent to MacMahon that place was indistinguishable from the people who lived there, so that places such as the town, the street, the square and the river are inevitably linked with the occupants of these areas, who had an enormous influence on his writing:

> Men and women were on all sides about me, some of them lonely, unloved and unappreciated, perhaps, others brave in heroic deeds of battling adversity, others again aspiring, defeated or successful, ambitious, sullen, rancorous, sublimated, treacherous and loyal by turns, devoted, ennobled, enslaved, or as the old quotation has it 'living lives of quiet desperation'. One man said 'it takes all kinds to make a world' and in reply a cranky neighbour shouted meaningfully 'and they're all there too!!' All were human, each was unique. How to convey to others these moments or flickers of uniqueness, these epiphanies of the passing day, tinctured by the

virtues and vices this transference connotes. A writer goes around the world, whoring after strange gods: he then returns to his own place, observes something simple that moves him profoundly; this he sets down on papers accurately, sensitively and with balance. There and then he has literature (from *The Storyman*).

MacMahon looked about him and down at the ground at his feet 'one does not search for diamonds with a telescope'. As the Irish expression has it: 'I put listening ears on myself, to isolate the precious core of what moved people.'

Dan Flavin, the bookshop owner, Bob Cuthbertson, the printer, Seamus Wilmot, a teacher, the Bunyan brothers, the blacksmiths, Moss Scanlon, the harnessmaker and Brown Paddy known as old Brown who in turn was a bookmaker, butcher, publican, county councillor and a gambler, all had an enormous influence on the works of Bryan MacMahon.

These were personalities in his town whom he knew and loved. Nowadays they would be called 'characters' but he preferred to call them 'personalities' as the dictionary defines a personality as a remarkable person, one who, by extension of the sum of his parts, adds up to the unique. Yes, he would agree they were all engaging, entertaining, informative, eccentric, amusing and unusual – indeed they were unique! In a small, tightly-knit community such as his own town there was no shortage of personalities coming in all sorts and sizes of many attitudes, oddities and hues. These personalities also had great mental capacity and imagination, with that quality of coherence of belonging which sets loneliness to flight and keeps body, mind and soul together.

Friendship in a small community is of the essence – to have people with whom you feel fully at home, who by intuition can sense your various mood swings (and you theirs) and make allowance therefore. This is an absolute necessity for those who live in a small town; of such a place it may truly be said that the houses have walls of glass. The extract below is from the recently published work, *Hero Town*, by MacMahon and sums up how he felt about his community:

> Hero Town he called it. What the hell is heroic about it? Are all its citizens brave and admirable? Good God – no. Of what then does their heroism consist? They are truly human. They understand human relationships. They preserve social equipoise. If a man raises his head in pride they lower it: If he lowers it they raise it. It's an unarticulated law. It is handed down. Without courts. The people have familiars, totems and taboos. They preserve the life of the imagination. They communicate in the shorthand of the nerves.

However, if there is one quotation that sums up the influences of people and place on Bryan MacMahon's works it is one from Hillare Belloc:

> From humble homes and first beginnings
> Out to the undiscovered ends
> There is nothing worth the wear of winning
> But laughter and love of friends.

Hero Town is right – a good description.

CHAPTER TWO

The Glitterin' Man:
Bryan MacMahon as Storyteller

Bernard O'Donoghue

Bryan MacMahon's celebrated first memoir *The Master* (Poolbeg, 1992) had the perfect name for the famous writer-schoolteacher's autobiography. On the first page of his second memoir, *The Storyman* (Poolbeg, 1994) MacMahon tells us why he chose that title for it. It is *The Storyman* because 'in one form or another my whole life has been devoted to the telling of stories'.* He is, before all else, a storyteller. 'Teller' is the operative element here: MacMahon is universally recognised as one of the great Irish short-story writers of the twentieth century – which, we must remember, was also the heyday of the form. The short-story is (for reasons pondered by Frank O'Connor in *The Lonely Voice*) the most successful literary form in Irish English: the form that the Irish writer has been most at home in since 1900 with James Joyce and George Moore. But, in ways that most of his fellow short-story writers – his competitors in the form, you might say – were not, he was also a story-teller, both in person and on the page. As master-writer of the short-story he has affinities with the Russian masters Chekhov and Gogol, and the Cork masters O'Connor and Ó Faoláin, and with the greatest master of all, Joyce. But he has affinities too with the oral seanchaí Eamonn Kelly. As his invention of the epoch-making radio programme *The Rambling House* would suggest, he himself was also a seanchaí who understood and appreciated the activity of the teller of stories, familiar and unfamiliar.

What I want to do here is to try to define the distinctive excellence of MacMahon's short-stories, mostly concentrating on a few of his classic anthology-pieces. But first of all I want to dwell a bit further on the term 'storyteller', returning to the title of *The Storyman*. MacMahon tells us at the start how it came about as a term applied to him by a boy in the street, saying that he liked the term 'storyman' straight away because of its parallel to things like 'seaman, clergyman ... oarsman ... milkman, foreman, penman and perhaps even conman' (p.1).

Particularly, the reader is tempted to suggest, conman. MacMahon's writing, like his conversation, is full of conmen. It is a typical MacMahon sleight of hand to end the above list with that significant term, and then sweep on with his narrative before slyly returning to the activities of a confidence-man in what he calls 'the university of the marketplace' (p.26) to end chapter one. He is interested in cons and conmen because of course the storyman, the fiction-writer, is above all else a conman. If writers of fiction do not con their audience, they fail. We have to believe them, even though we know they are making it all up. It is a point that MacMahon returns to again and again. On the second page of *The Storyman* he says, describing the strange events at the market in Listowel in his childhood, 'I don't expect to be believed when I say that there were dancing bears from Russia and dancing ducks from anywhere at all'. Why doesn't he expect to be believed? Of course we do believe him in this case: it sounds true; and what would be the point of saying it if it wasn't true? *The Storyman* is a memoir, so it is telling the truth even if it is a truth suitably embroidered by the skilled pen of the story-writer.

But most of the time MacMahon is the storyman, the fiction maker who is himself the conman, at liberty to make things up and whose task it is to persuade the reader of the reality of what is unreal. The point is made with great explicitness in one of his best-known stories, used for the title of one of his most admired volumes of stories, *The Lion-Tamer*. The narrator goes to a pub in a village in which he is a stranger. It begins credibly enough with the narrator saying 'I am gregarious and convivial to a degree considered alarming by my friends' (p.1). Everyone who had the good fortune to know Bryan MacMahon personally will recognise this narrator as not that far from his convivial creator: this, it would seem, is not an unreliable narrator or whatever critical term is used for that. We can trust the author here. He falls into conversation with the only other pub customer, an uncommunicative character, decidedly ungregarious and unconvivial, the opposite of the friendly narrator, his antitype even. Gradually thawing, this sole drinker challenges the narrator to guess his profession. When our narrator gives up, he is told that his addresser is 'the only Irish-born lion-tamer'; and when he silently betrays some scepticism:

> He was quick to resent the fact that, in my own mind, I was calling him a liar.
>
> 'If you doubt my word,' he snapped, 'I shall ask our friend O'Donoghue'. He swivelled in his chair to ask the publican to bear witness for him, but Mr O'Donoghue had vanished into the back premises from whence the clinking of bottles came to our ears. I hastened to reassure him that I fully believed him.

The lion-tamer goes on to relate in minute circumstantial detail his extraordinary and terrifying experiences, culminating in his confrontation with a lioness while drunk and nauseous with whiskey. The story is full of picturesque and explicit detail: the lion-tamer's predecessor had noted that there were only three lion-tamers in Ireland, 'one of them in the city of Derry and he crippled with arthritis' (p.6). Later in the story this detail is misquoted as 'crippled with rheumatism' (p.8) and is rapidly corrected by the main narrator in the story to 'arthritis', vouching for the convincing consistency of the narrative. At the end of the compelling story the lion-tamer abruptly leaves the pub as 'a clock struck': like Cinderella, or the ghost of Hamlet's father (p.16). Our narrator orders a nightcap and falls into conversation with the landlord, O'Donoghue:

> 'Isn't he good?' he asked.
>   'Damn good!' I agreed.
>   'What was it?'
>   'Eh?'
>   'It wasn't the Lizard in the Cardinal's Pocket?' The man's eyes pipped in anticipation of tiny triumph.
>   'Eh? No no.'
>   'Let me think. Don't tell me. Was it the Litter of Elk-Hounds he sold in Cruft's?'
>   'He said he was a lion-tamer,' I faltered.
>   The publican grew solemn; then wan. Suddenly he brightened in parochial pride. 'Blast me if I ever heard that one before' ... He ruminated for a moment. Then his face splintered into the joy of discovery. 'Blast me if it isn't Miss Evans' cats.' (p.16)

And he goes on to explain that this storyteller always invented a story and persona that was suggested by a recent trivial experience (the lizard was suggested by 'a kid who brought a frog to school in his handkerchief' [p.16], and so on. Where, we are tempted to ask, did Bryan MacMahon, the teacher, get that episode from? Is the lion-tamer the schoolmaster?)

The more you ponder the story of the lion-tamer and its interlinked prevarications, the more brilliantly intricate it becomes. Who exactly is being conned here? The narrator is conned with great effectiveness: for example by the way that the lion-tamer narrator corrects minor inconsistencies like the arthritis, enlisting the listener's memory of the details in support of his credibility. The narrator is well taken in, and rejoices in the end at the fact that 'in this shabby insignificant hollow in Ireland' he has encountered this 'reincarnated spirit of Munchausen' (Baron Munchausen was an eighteenth-century German soldier who invented legendarily exaggerated stories of his achievements and experiences).

But when you think about it further, this isn't just a story in which a casual acquaintance pretends to have been a lion-tamer. There are all kinds of claims and improbabilities. The lion-tamer enlists in support of his veracity not only our memory but also a landlord called O'Donoghue, having carefully checked that he is out of earshot and his appeal for corroboration cannot be heard. Is the landlord's name really O'Donoghue? We don't know. And of course it doesn't matter. He is just a character in a story. Is the lion-tamer's name Moran (from which the ringmaster derives his highly improbable circus name 'Moranni)? Is one more real than the other?

But what *do* we know anyway as readers? And what does it matter in fiction? We know what the writer chooses to tell us; and in this story he comes very close to telling us that we can't believe daylight from him. His conman lion-tamer is quick to resent scepticism or the charge that he is a liar (which is putting it strongly). But the storyman here is cheerfully and cunningly ready to put us on the wrong track. Every observation of the lion-tamer about Birmingham, we are told at the start, was 'objective, terse and accurate' (p.2); obviously, it seems, a man whose account can be trusted. The outer narrator tells us 'I thought he seemed inclined to bear away from the absorbing subject of lion-taming' (p.3) so the reader/audience would deduce that this man is reluctant to tell of his experiences taming lions. Could anything be further from the truth? And what has become of my claim that this is not an unreliable narrator, or my observation that the gregarious and convivial narrator sounds very like Bryan MacMahon? The writer has run rings round us; we are fooled as effectively as the victims of the little confidence-man behind his table at the end of chapter one of *The Storyman*. As MacMahon says at the end of that tale of trickery: 'Gullibility!' (p.26)

Because of course from the reader's viewpoint a young pub acquaintance who pretends to have been a lion-tamer is no nearer or further from the truth than a writer who makes up a story about a pub acquaintance who pretends to have been a lion-tamer. I have dwelt at length on this story for a number of reasons: first, it is a theme – the question of reality and invention – that MacMahon returns to insistently in his stories. The story that most fully parallels it is that masterpiece of the seanchaí tradition 'The Glitterin' Man'. Here the sceptical hearer is ruthlessly, and very successfully, destroyed by being drawn into the story as an alter ego of the devil. Micky Doyle 'the half-poet' (and I will return to this figure in the general context of MacMahon later) is telling a story at a wake. It is the familiar folktale of the gambler who plays cards against the devil, recognising him by a glance at his 'cloven huffs'. The story is so familiar that the listeners are hardly listening; this doesn't trouble the storyteller much, but he takes offence at the more overt scepticism of Edmond Heffernan, a substantial farmer who is 'sneering audibly'. The teller suddenly incorporates him into the story by getting the other listeners to stare at the farmer's feet to see if they are cloven, by way of illustration. The farmer's anger is at once mysterious and psychologically convincing. As with 'The Lion-Tamer', we feel that scepticism is liable to be punished as a crime against the artist who can, if he chooses, show us how it is done. But we mustn't presume to see through the mysterious art if we are not invited to or beware the skills of the conman! The reader is represented in the story by the listeners at the wake.

A second reason that I dwelt so extensively on 'The Lion-Tamer' was to note that its lifting of the fictive veil is not something shared with other Irish short-story writers who tend to keep to the demands of a more literal kind of naturalism. As it happens, MacMahon's practice here has a good deal in common with non-Irish modern theories of fictionality. The favourite modern practitioner of the kind of story that admits to its own fictiveness is the Italian novelist Italo Calvino, particularly in his strange, sceptical novel *If on a winter's night a traveller*, where the operative word is 'if'. Calvino too concedes that the story is just make-believe, told 'for the sake of argument'. That 'if' means 'just supposing'. In reality of course all fiction begins implicitly 'just supposing'.

Most distantly maybe, the English writer who famously pursues this intricate narrative scepticism is Chaucer; this kind of revelation of a writer's procedures was very popular in the Middle Ages. The 'Pardoner's Tale', in which the disgraceful pardoner tells the other pilgrims on the way to Canterbury that his relics are all a sham – an old piece of cloth that he claims is Our Lady's veil; pig's bones masquerading as a saint's relics, and the like – but that he can preach of damnation and hell-fire with such eloquence that his audience will believe him anyway. Again, it is the conman as artist. The artistic subterfuge may not always be as nasty as the pardoner's story of greed and violence; earlier in Chaucer's century Dante says a poem is a *bella mensogna*, a beautiful lie. The crucial concession is that art is a lie of one sort or another. This medieval view is much more evident in the Irish tradition than in most European literatures: MacMahon's conman of course is typical of the Irish *cleasaí*, the trickster, who also makes a sudden appearance in Boucicault's nineteenth-century *Shaughraun*.

It is easy to find in MacMahon's work other instances of the same concerns we have seen in 'The Lion-Tamer'. For instance, the unreliable narrator in 'Yung Mari Li' suddenly says, 'Now, I cannot tell you with any degree of accuracy what the priest said to his people' (p.50). Why not, we may well ask, since he is making it all up. He can be as accurate – or of course as in-accurate – as he likes. Chaucer comes to mind again: in the prologue to *The Canterbury Tales*, the narrator says with appa-rent anxiety: 'don't blame me if some of these characters speak a bit crudely; anyone who reports what a man says has to use that man's words, however objectionable they may be.' But of course the author has total power to change or dictate what a man says, since he is inventing him in the first place.

It is instructive to consider this practice of MacMahon's – the narrator as ingenious conman – in relation to other ex-ponents of the Irish short-story. He is not a naturalist, I think, despite the power with which he evokes and incorporates into his stories local characters and languages. His work is rarely predictable, despite its rootedness in the locality. Frank O'Connor is an obvious contrast. To read a great O'Connor story, like 'The Luceys' or 'The Mad Lomasneys' is to get to know a group of people: people with whom we could make a guess at how they would act outside the confines of the story (though there are also great O'Connor stories, like 'The Majesty of the Law' that do belong in recognisable MacMahon territory). But one of the reasons that it is possible to misread MacMahon's stories at the moment is that the recent masters of the form in Ireland – pre-eminently McGahern and Trevor perhaps – are highly naturalistic. MacMahon's celebration of the oddness of the world requires some readjustment in the receiver.

It might too seem a disservice to work that is as rooted in its own place and language as MacMahon's is to subject it to this kind of scrutiny. But I think we do not do it justice if we fail to see that in his composition there is a great deal of sophistication quietly at work. It is evident on every page that the work is not only vital and rooted; it is also very highly crafted. One of the great accolades to MacMahon is quoted on the back of *The Storyman* and in many other places: a letter from Seán Ó Faoláin, perceptively saluting MacMahon as a kind of prose-poet. 'You have written short-stories based on common life in the mood of a prose-poet ... the wonder of it to pedestrian prose-writers like me ... is that you have created as a result an extra art dimension.' It is a very handsome tribute, and a large claim, but I think it is identifying precisely what MacMahon's achievement is. The art is what needs to be stressed because he operates, I think to an almost unparalleled degree, in a vernacular world at the point at which it is turning into art.

Any analysis of the language will show this. Taking a sentence almost at random, here is a passage from 'The Clarinet':

> [He] hung the tin on the spear of a Gold Flake sign. He sat on his grug on the top step with his legs pulled up to him. He wetted his lips with a gentle relish as if he were enjoying the bouquet of a rare wine. He put the instrument to his lips and was appeased and pleased when he had brought the mouthpiece to his own mouth's heat. (LT [lion-tamer], p.26)

The Gold Flake sign economically locates the story in place and time. Then the word 'grug' localises it further: maybe as narrowly as to north Kerry. So, if it is true that MacMahon was a graduate of 'the university of the ordinary people' (*The Storyman* [p.10]) and that Liam Ó Muirthile's great formulation 'náisiún na mbailte fearann' ('the nation of the townlands') from 'An Párlús' fits him well, his thematic realm also extends further. This is why the stories often turn on a mysterious phrase, and often use that phrase for their title. This happens, for example, in 'Gentlemen, this is Armageddon', that strange story in which a trio of showfolk (again) visit their settled sister and her baby. The title comes from a meaningless jingle that features in the trio's new act; but no attempt is made to explain its significance in this strange context. What we find is a very clear situation: this glamorous showgirl Nanette has married a farmer and been reduced to a kind of drudgery, made more acute by a bitter and bullying mother-in-law. But it is not clear whether or not she is better off than the trio who are moving into unglamorous old age in the show life. And into this very stark setting MacMahon has injected the curious, unmeaning mantra of the title.

The most famous example of this unexplained naming is a

story which is in almost all anthologies of the Irish short-story, 'Ballinteerna in the Morning'. This is the wonderful story of a country hare (all hares are from the country in origin), which ends up in the basement of a barber's shop in Dublin: the country/town opposition is crucial. In the story two young men, described in great but it seems unenlighting detail, arrive to repair a country creamery. A boy leads them across the bog and on the way captures a hare from its form. One of the young men, apparently with a formed but undescribed purpose, brings it back to Dublin and releases it in O'Connell Street. The hare bolts down the steps of a barber's shop where it is approached by Richard Collis, the head barber. Both hare and barber are described in purely visual terms: the hare is like a child's drawing of a hare, and his body is composed visually of three ovals. Even more strangely, we are told that Collis' skull has the shape of an inflated pig's bladder, and that 'his complexion, though a trifle over scarlet, was undoubtedly first class' (contrasting perhaps with that of one of the young men who is albino). Oddest of all, we are told that 'the points of his moustache were his twin-treasures and compensated in some measure for a childless marriage' (pp.37–8). He kneels before the hare who reacts first with friendliness and then with apathy, and he exclaims 'Wisha God be with you, Ballinteerna in the morning!' (p.39) The story says: 'High in his mind the years clinked by like silver beads.'

That is all we are told. The narration itself acknowledges the barber-shop hare/hair pun. There are other thematic echoes: for instance in the bog 'a not repulsive odour of old sulphur came up out of the mould underfoot' (p.31) whereas the barber's shop 'had a repulsive smell compounded of superannuated combs and hair-oil in semi-rusty tins'. Clearly there is nothing as crude as a moral in this brilliantly surreal narrative; but the

natural in the country seems to be not 'repulsive' in a way that
the urban and artificial-cosmetic is. But I think what is most
distinctive about MacMahon's view of the local is that be believes – and demonstrates – that there is as much of the surprising and the artistic in local traditions as in the officially recognised art-world. It is the demonstration of this that needs details which are eccentric, surreal and unexplained. MacMahon's
view of the rural is the opposite of primitivist. What is age-old
is not necessarily without sophistication. Indeed MacMahon's
tendency towards a ringingly optimistic conclusion to his stories
of country traditions implies that the opposite more likely.

A MacMahon story which seems to belong squarely in the
rural seanchaí's tradition but is also concerned with the im-
pingement of the new upon the old is also one of the most
admired and anthologised, and again features as title a ringing
but inexact phrase: 'The Good Dead in the Green Hills'. It is
another instance of the interlocking of the familiar and the
unfamiliar, the local and the eccentric. This story does bear
some resemblance to another celebrated Irish short-story,
Seamus O'Kelly's 'The Weaver's Grave'. Peadar Feeney is the
storyteller, holding court every night in the house of Tommyo
who is stone-blind and 'as old as an eagle'. The stories ascribed
to Peadar are a mixture of the familiar ('The King of Ireland's
Son') and the unfamiliar ('The Loaf in the Mare's Ear', 'The
Earl of Banemore' and 'Shower of Old Hags': a list that reminds
us of the heterogeneity of the lion-tamer's tall stories). Peadar
withdraws in bitterness from the nightly gatherings at Tommyo's
when the wireless arrives, putting him out of business as he sees
it. 'The radio and the story-teller made sorry bedmates' (p.138),
in the words of the story. For the most part Peadar is unmissed;
but one night in a fit of conscience Tommyo sends the boy-

narrator to try to persuade him back. When he delivers his
message, Peadar disconcertingly replies 'Spell Constantinople'.
When the messenger cannot spell it, the old man triumphantly
cries out 'Who's right now?' (p.139), and gives his answer to
the message: 'First tell him that if the messenger is cold the
answer is cold, and secondly tell him that under the watchful
eye of the Sweet Man Above (here Peadar raised his hat) the
Good Dead are alive in the Green Hills.' When the boy reports
this back to Tommyo, 'Tommyo took the strange message with
considerable gravity. He raised his eyes and said, "A bed in
Heaven to them that are gone before us all, and let Him who
made us unmake us." He sent for Peadar no more.' (p.140)

When Peadar's 'queer sister' dies he is moved to the County
Home, twenty-five miles away. In due course he dies too and
his neighbours of the lane (the locale of course of many of
MacMahon's stories) get together at Tommyo's to talk about it.
There is outrage that Peadar has not been buried after three
days, and a deputation is sent to bring the body back. After
various objections and improvements enforced by Tommyo
(mountings for the coffin and so on) they conclude by opening
the coffin to ensure it is the right corpse, and he is ready for
burial. In a passage irresistibly reminiscent of Synge's *Riders to
the Sea*, we learn that 'They put the good brown socks on his
feet and ... it was Tommyo who pulled the new rich kype down
over the face' (p.150). The story ends with an assertion of good-
ness: 'The funeral was a good one, even though the clothes of
some of the mourners were soiled with dung and feathers and
blood' (p.150). And finally, led by the blind man who does not
observe the traditional halts, the narrator finds himself in an
isolated group of four at the head of the funeral, and brings the
story to an astonishingly positive – even fearlessly sentimental

– conclusion: 'At first I felt ashamed, then suddenly pride began to choke me when I realised I was the leader of all those beautiful people.' The conclusive word 'beautiful' is so surprising as to be startling.

This story, with its sweepingly positive ending, centres on the traditional and the local. Evidence of MacMahon's aesthetic is to be found in the description of the mourners 'soiled with dung and feathers and blood'. It is a detail that risks bathos; it is on the verge of farce. It brings us back to the place where MacMahon offers us his organic theory of art, in chapter one of *The Storyman* again:

> All art, I tell myself, comes up out of the clay. Out of the cow-dung if needs be. It is refined, projected, and later imitated or developed in the city where, for a time, it blooms like a flower. The flower becomes a seed-pod which explodes and scatters its seeds … With luck, each seed comes to rest on a fertile plot and there renews its life-cycle once again. This theory I apply to literature. (pp.15–16)

This says a great deal about the relationship between art and the local. It is a similar theory to Patrick Kavanagh's much-invoked opposition between the parochial, which is good, and the provincial, which is bad. MacMahon too believes that what comes without apology or modification out of the parish is good; it knows its own rules. But what he does characteristically is to refuse to break open the pod of meaning in the local plant; there is always something (like the significance of Ballinteerna) held back as the precious possession of the locality itself, something which cannot be reprocessed for the outside world. The writer he most resembles here is Seamus Heaney whose poem 'Broagh' says the title-word's final 'gh' is a sound that 'the strangers find difficult to manage'. Like MacMahon's elusive phrases and titles, it remains a property of the local parish.

Ó Faoláin is right when he says that this peculiar quality is more typically a property of the poem, whether in prose or not. And of course a highly significant part of MacMahon's achievement was as a poet and balladeer. Hence his love of all languages: Irish of all dialects; the traveller language shelta; and above all English in all its registers, from the romantic poetic of the closing stanzas of 'The Valley of Knockanure':

The golden sun is setting now behind the Feale and Lee;
The pale, pale moon is rising far out beyond Tralee,
The dismal stars and clouds afar are darkened o'er the moor

to the perfectly caught balladeering language of 'Christy Ring':

'The hay is saved and Cork are bate'
all round the cry does ring.
You speak too soon, my sweet garsún,
For here comes Christy Ring.

There are instances too of legal register as in that wonderfully sinister story 'The Breadmaker'. So we do not exhaust Mac-Mahon's resources – his conman's box of tricks – by looking at his predecessors and contemporaries in the short-story. He has a wider compass than any of them: or at least he draws on more materials to put them together. MacMahon's fondness for introducing without explanation a dialect or Irish word into his English weave anticipates a whole school of modern poets in English (Paulin, Heaney, Longley).

So where might we look, beyond the traditional Irish short-story whose bounds MacMahon often goes outside, for parallels? To begin with, the inclination towards the surreal and the linguistically bizarre has striking North Kerry affinities, of which the most undeniable – and here I think there is a direct influence – is with the playwright George Fitzmaurice. The ability to make the surreal piercingly human is characteristic of Fitzmaurice, in *The Dandy Dolls* in particular maybe, dealing with the obsessed artist-figure who is so pervasive in Mac-Mahon's work. Indeed this surrealist inclination towards a kind of reckless abandon in portraying the non-naturalistic is a significant sub-theme in the North Kerry writers; MacMahon's pupil Seán McCarthy is a further example.

There are also affinities beyond Ireland. MacMahon is a remarkable blend of the locally rooted and the cosmopolitan. I mentioned already the Italian novelist, Italo Calvino, who is often seen in the vanguard of postmodernist fiction; the comparison with MacMahon can be extended. Calvino collected a huge body of Italian folktales, exactly the same kind of narratives which are the stock-in-trade of the seanchaí (they are published by Faber in a thick volume of 700 pages – sadly in a poor translation). The titles bear out this oral link with the seanchaí: 'The King of Denmark's Son', 'The Happy Man's Shirt' and so on. But what is most strikingly in common is the clarity and simplicity of narrative line, often combined with the surreal. Obviously there is no question of direct influence here, but two points might be made. First, this movement to incorporate folk-elements into the central cultural canon – in poetry, music, stories and everywhere – is a major development in the arts in the early twentieth century, associated with Bartok and Janacek as much as writers of the Celtic Revival like Yeats. MacMahon reflects this more forcefully than any of his Irish contemporaries, suggesting a kind of paradox: that the use of local materials is itself cosmopolitan as a practice.

Passing mention might be made of comparisons within English fiction. The marked sexual element in some of the stories recalls D. H. Lawrence: the almost pantheistic sense of pulsing life in which MacMahon often exults in is reminiscent of *The Rainbow*, and the strange connection of horses with female maturity in 'Chestnut and Jet' brings to mind 'St Mawr', the novella so much admired by F. R. Leavis. Female sexuality is also a Lawrentian theme in two stories included in the 1985 collection *The Sound of Hooves:* 'The Right to be Maudlin' and the astonishing 'A Woman's Hair'. The same tendency towards the symbolic is evident in stories such as 'The Ring' (I have already noted the reminiscence of Synge in symbolic objects; he is also brought to mind by the beautiful story 'An Island Funeral' in *The Sound of Hooves*). The kind of symbolic anti-quarianism that parallels Synge also links MacMahon with Steinbeck: for example the instinctive brutality of Pompey Connors in 'Black Nets' ('Whenever he put down his boot he churlishly saw to it that he placed it on a shrivelled daisy or a winsome heartsease') recalls in its primitivism the famous opening of *The Grapes of Wrath* when Tom Joad nearly swerves off the road in his attempt to hit the turtle that a woman driver has just nearly plunged to her death trying to avoid.

With these links I am trying to suggest the wide range of a writer that Benedict Kiely called 'probably the most richly endowed of Irish writers'. But the essence of Bryan MacMahon's achievement lies in the fact that his imagination is much more anarchic than most of his contemporaries. His people are real people, but they are also odd. Frank O'Connor's view of the short-story that it was a 'lonely voice' – the product of an individualistic writer at the margins of a cultural tradition – is not quite right for MacMahon who is a kind of society-centred symbolist rather than an isolated imagist. The Russian formalist idea of defamiliarisation perhaps fits him best: his materials are familiar, yet the constructs he makes out of them force us to see them in a new way, often in forms that we can't quite grasp.

From considering what this short-story writer does with his artistry – the dazzling cons that he often performs on the reader – we might move on finally to ponder what the short-story in general typically does. MacMahon considers the issue very explicitly in the story 'The Egotists' (the title is equivalent to 'the artists'). The narrator wants to see 'the boy-hero's wounds', but in explaining his interest he considers the merits of various literary forms. 'After all, what is the poem but a literary corset? Form plus figure minus comfort ... But the short-story? The short-story is no sop on the road ... I can utilise the expressions I've filched from the people's mouths, juggle them with a few of my own compositions, and who'll be the wiser?' (p.101) It is the conman again, exploiting what is around him. Indeed his practice is precisely like that of the 'little confidence-man' in *The Storyman* who persuades his audience to spend a pound to buy back their own pound (p.26). 'The Egotists' ends with a competition in tall stories, about whose brother has died more lamentably. It is clear that it is a competition in tallness rather than veracity.

One of the most memorable images in *The Irish Times* and other Irish papers in recent years showed the five sons of Bryan MacMahon walking with his coffin. There was no mistaking this as a national moment of the first importance: one of the country's leading writers and communicators had died. To see quite how well-placed this veneration and sense of national loss were we need to examine again the details of Bryan Mac-Mahon's achievement. He has something of the half-poet like Micky Doyle in 'The Glitterin' Man' (as well as a metrically gifted whole poet); but the other and more important half is a magic-weaving composer and writer of stories. And, even if he does sometimes let us see how his spells are cast, in 'The Lion-Tamer' or 'The Egotists', his greatest and most characteristic achievement lies in the secrets of his mystery, the tricks that he does not impart, like the location of Ballinteerna. His art is obsessed with the unreachable at the heart of the local and the personal.

* I am only footnoting two books in this essay: *The Storyman* (1994) and the early collection of short-stories *The Lion-Tamer* (1948; quoted from the 1995 edition by Souvenir Press, London and Canada). I have put page references to those books in the text when it seemed useful.

CHAPTER THREE

The Master *in Context: Bryan MacMahon and Other Literary Masters and Mistresses (and of the Vagaries of Literary Reputation)*

Jo O'Donoghue

It goes without saying that Ireland is coming down with literary masters and mistresses and has done so as long as anyone can remember: think of Peadar O'Donnell, Roddy Doyle, Patrick McCabe, Ita Daly, Catherine Dunne, Gabriel Fitzmaurice – to name a tiny number. When educational opportunities were scarce in the first half of the twentieth century, the training college was one of the few escape routes for the bright girl or (more usually) boy from a rural background. 'Educated at St Patrick's Training College, Drumcondra, Dublin' is the mantra of the biographies of writers in both Irish and English: John McGahern, Francis MacManus, Máirtín Ó Cadhain, Seosamh Mac Grianna, Séamus Ó Grianna, Donncha Ó Céileachair, Aindrias Ó Muimhneacháin, Críostóir Ó Floinn, Pádraig Ó Siochfhradha. Some of these teachers lost their jobs: for political reasons, like Ó Cadhain; because they fell foul of clerical displeasure, like Ó Floinn or McGahern; or they left, like Ó Céileachair, to work on Tomás de Bhaldraithe's dictionary or to become an editor for An Gúm or to take up a position in RTÉ, like MacManus. Bryan MacMahon took the same route to St

Patrick's Drumcondra, returned to teach in Listowel in 1931 at the age of twenty-one and, unlike many of the others, remained both a teacher and in Listowel until his retirement in 1975 and the end of his life, respectively.[1]

From this *embarras de richesses* of literary masters and mistresses I have chosen one male and one female writer of fiction to counterpoint Bryan MacMahon. Francis MacManus (1909–65) was an exact contemporary of MacMahon. Kate O'Brien (1897–1974) was born more than ten years earlier. The choice reflects my personal literary preferences and satisfies too the second criterion suggested in the title above: 'the vagaries of literary reputation'. MacManus and O'Brien are both underrated writers; MacManus is now unfashionable and little read.

Bryan MacMahon (1909–92) was a literary institution in Ireland, famed for his short-stories and, among reluctant students of Irish at any rate, for his translation of *Peig*.[2] The first books of his with which I was associated were the Patsy-O titles of the late 1980s, which were published by Poolbeg Press in Dublin when I was editorial director there.[3] In a published piece on MacMahon, Gabriel Fitzmaurice reports the author as saying that he had written the Patsy-O books 'with his left hand' and opines that they were not of the same high standard as other books he wrote for children, notably *Jockomoora* and *The King of Ireland's Son*.[4] I felt that they were dated, laboured and didactic and thought it likely that he had written them some time previously and had supplied them to us in response to a request from Philip MacDermott of Poolbeg. Later, when I reread *The Master*, I noticed a reference to Patsy-O which, although unspecific, appears to date from the 1950s, when Éamon Kelly was still living in Listowel and he and Bryan went in search of stories from a seanchaí in south-west Kerry: 'About this time too, possibly because of a seminal anecdote by the south-west Kerry storyteller, I invented a character called Patsy-O, an impish boy who had five wonderful pets.'[5] The next sentence, however, suggests that the genesis of Patsy-O was somewhat later: 'I had tried out some of these stories on the pupils in the school or in the garden of my son's house, surrounded by my grandchildren and their friends on the occasion of a birthday party.'(p.65)

I remember, too, *The Master* landing on my desk. It was a very long typescript in a box and it had to be vigorously pruned for publication (not by me but by a freelance editor, Séamas Ó Brógáin). I heard later on from another Irish publisher that he too had had it on his desk but had turned it down because it was too long and unwieldy and required too much work. Luck favoured Poolbeg; we brought the book out in hardback for the autumn–Christmas market of 1992. I was at the Frankfurt Book Fair in October when I heard that it was doing very well and was about to be reprinted. Gay Byrne had had Bryan MacMahon on his morning radio programme for MacMahon's birthday – he was eighty-three that autumn – and said it was 'a smashing book'. And it ran and ran.

The Master and the posthumously published *Hero Town* are the only MacMahon books still in print, although his short-stories and other works, as well as a second volume of autobiography, *The Storyman*, were published or reissued by Poolbeg at a great rate in the mid-1990s, after I left the company: *The Storyman*, 1994; *The Tallystick*, 1994; *Children of the Rainbow*, *The Sound of Hooves* and *The Honeyspike*, all in 1995; and a final collection of short-stories which, I believe, reached the shops the month of MacMahon's death, in February 1998: *A*

Final Fling: Conversations between Men and Women. Almost the whole decade of the 1990s was, in publishing terms, a final fling, a late flowering, a blaze of glory, for Bryan MacMahon. And it all started with *The Master*.

Many writers of Bryan MacMahon's age or even much younger – I mean writers of quality – live to see their books become unfashionable, remain unfashionable and stay stubbornly out of print. Kate O'Brien published her last novel, *As Music and Splendour*, in 1958, although she produced two further works of non-fiction, *My Ireland* (1962) and the autobiographical *Presentation Parlour* (1963). It was known that she was working on another novel, with the Austen-like title of *Constancy*, for many years but she never completed it. When she died in Kent in 1974 she had very little money and none of her books was in print. Douglas Gageby (1918–2004), then editor of the *Irish Times*, had continued to commission a column from her and a cheque from that newspaper was one of the last she endorsed, shortly before her death.

Francis MacManus died prematurely in 1965. His last novel, *The Fire in the Dust*, was published in 1950, not long after he left teaching for the features department of RTÉ. He published books until the end of his life – he wrote in Irish, he wrote biographies and he edited collections of the RTÉ Thomas Davis lectures series, which he had initiated. One of the finest of these, *The Years of the Great Test*, was published in 1966, the year after his death. MacManus had a wide readership and considerable influence when he was first published but scarcely anyone reads him now and not a single work of his is in print. Mercier Press did its best to revive an interest in him, reissuing several of his novels in the 1960s; and Poolbeg Press under the editorial leadership of David Marcus reissued *Watergate* (1942) in 1980. *Men Withering* and *The Greatest of These*, two novels from his historical trilogy of the 1930s, were an unpopular prescription on the secondary school curriculum until the 1980s. Now you will find MacManus' works, mainly in Talbot Press hardback editions of the 1930s and 1940s, in libraries, second-hand bookshops or on the bookshelves of the occasional parish priest – for MacManus, unlike Kate O'Brien, was acceptable to the censorious mid-twentieth-century Catholic mindset. Perhaps his reputation suffered because he was one of the few Irish writers of quality never to have been banned by the Censorship of Publications Board.

'Beloved claustrophobia of small-town Ireland' – Bryan MacMahon and *The Master*

The vision of *The Master* is essentially a comic and ameliorative one, conveying the sense that most things are for the best and that things that are not satisfactory can over time and with some effort be improved and made satisfactory. Perhaps it is this lightness of tone that made the book so popular, particularly among practising teachers, for nowadays – if a former teacher can risk an opinion – it seems not to be an optimistic profession.

For example two important issues are raised in the opening pages which, even before they are discussed, are downplayed by being linked with the comic set-piece of the ferret in the canon's sitting-room. The first is the issue of clerical power to hire and fire teachers while answering to nobody. If the clergy could have been trusted to act with justice all or even some of the time this power to hire and fire, to make or break people on a whim, might not have had such serious consequences. But an abuse of power will always lead to more abuses of power and so it was for clerical school managers in Ireland until well into the second half of the twentieth century. The second is the generational dispute between the young Bryan MacMahon and his mother, herself a teacher in Listowel and the means of acquiring the teaching post for young Bryan. 'Patiently, my mother wore me down' (p.2), is how he summarises her persuasion and his yielding. The issue is given no special significance in the even tenor of the opening pages: he was in Dublin, he wanted to stay in Dublin but he has now found himself back teaching in Listowel. Later we learn that the even younger Bryan had different ideas about the career he wanted to pursue; again his mother stepped in to prevail on him to sit the King's Scholarship examination for entry to St Patrick's Training College. Perhaps it is difficult after the passage of many decades for the writer to recall the feelings of anger and frustration that might have accompanied such wholesale thwarting of his wishes; any such feelings are certainly not evident in the book.

The memoir presents one teacher's view of his own teaching career, after the event – many decades after the event in some cases. There is no doubting his revulsion at the appalling standard of school accommodation and sanitation when he first began to teach in Listowel – and perhaps this information is necessary for readers born since the 1960s, who would themselves have no experience of conditions such as these. It is possible, when reading *The Master*, to overlook the fact that these appalling conditions persisted until 1959, the events of the two previous decades and the teachers' campaigns to improve conditions having been telescoped into one chapter of the book. As well as teaching itself, the Irish language, folklore and songs, sport, history and people were MacMahon's abiding interests and it seems that once he had relinquished the idea of returning to his first school in Dublin's South Circular Road, he found plenty to interest him in Listowel and its environs.

As he presents them in *The Master* MacMahon's energy and discipline are notable. Granted, his teacher's salary is nugatory and within a few years of his marriage he has to support five sons as well as a wife. Even so his industry seems phenomenal and the working day he describes leaves little room for leisure, or even for communing with his growing family. (At least there is no commuting time involved.) This is how he describes his day:

> From nine to three at school, hammer and tongs, with no drawing back. From three to four I ate my dinner and slept – the nap as a result of excellent advice I had received from an old schoolmaster, who counselled me always to let the sediment of the school day settle in the well of the mind. From four to nine I assisted or relieved my wife in the bookshop. From nine to ten I walked about the streets with my lifelong friend Ned Sheehy. At ten on the dot I sat at a table and wrote until one in the morning. This routine I kept up for the better part of fifteen years, and lived to tell the tale. (p.27)

Later (pp.108–9) he gives a further list of his extra-curricular activities, which include hurling, beagling, attending traditional gatherings such as Puck Fair, mastering Irish and Shelta, reading omnivorously and writing for literary magazines such as *The Bell*. The constant was the sleep between coming home from school and beginning the rest of his day.

As a teacher, Bryan MacMahon's constant focus is on unlocking creativity, promoting reading, with a little wizardry if necessary, opening what he calls the 'windows of wonder' to allow his pupils to 'explore this magic cave' of literature (p.52).

With the benefit of hindsight and given a viewpoint that is essentially optimistic, he recounts his successes in persuading reluctant boys to read. Even the hardened non-readers he gets around somehow, using all the resources of library, sport or community. Humour is never very far away; there are practical jokes, some of them verbal hoaxes, as when his boys give well-meaning visitors from the RSPCA exaggerated accounts of the mistreatment of animals in their homes and farms. And there is the incident when the sweep is sent by mischievous col-leagues to woo an unsuspecting woman teacher, for, as he says, 'school is nothing if it is not a place of laughter and song' (p.36). Many of the teachers who read this book over the past decade must have had a very different experience of primary education: of violent, embittered, disillusioned or fanatical teachers – teachers more akin to John Lee in Francis Mac-Manus' novel, *Flow On, Lovely River*, discussed below, than to the ebullient Bryan MacMahon. The author of *The Master* does make a passing reference to those teachers who 'lacking com-radely stimulus ... took to the bottle, to become eccentrics or alcoholics' (p.111) but in general he gives his colleagues a good press: 'As a group they loved Ireland and the things of Ireland, and were the pillars of the communities in which they taught' (p.111).

Even though MacMahon regularly left Listowel to lecture in the US and attend literary events he elected in the mid-1960s to return to 'the beloved claustrophobia of small-town Ireland' for the final ten years of his primary teaching career, rejecting offers of university positions in America. Among the reasons he gives are the reluctance of his wife but he also identifies the essential creative sustenance provided to him by his native town:

> But what would I without the Irish dimension to life – without the
> cut and thrust of banter, the laughter and the ballads, the summer
> playground of the west coast, the observance of the interplay and
> counterplay of local politics and intrigue, the mart-day meetings
> with country people, the in-for-a-chat of old friends and neigh-
> bours, the delightful discussion of books with my friend the retired
> librarian, the evening walks with Ned – all the minutiae of small-
> town living placed on the pan to balance that of material gain and
> superficial recognition. (p.187)

If writers are all egotists – and MacMahon claims they are ('For
a writer to claim that he is not an egotist is a contradiction'
[p.156]) – this writer clearly thought that to remain in Listowel
was his best means of serving and nourishing his creative gift.
Besides, no father of five children could have maintained such
a punishing schedule of work as well as a considerable creative
output without substantial support from his wife; perhaps his
deference to her wishes on the subject of going to live in
America was some recognition of her contribution.

Historian of Fine Conscience – two novels by Kate O'Brien
Kate O'Brien was born in Limerick, the Mellick of her novels,
a place she always loved – no Frank McCourt she – although
she lived for most of her adult life outside Ireland. She was
educated at Laurel Hill, a convent of the community of Faithful Companions of Jesus, or FCJ, as it is colloquially known, a
French order founded in 1844. Laurel Hill was known to Limerick people as the 'French convent' and is rendered in O'Brien's
novel *The Land of Spices* (1941) as the convent of the Com-
pagnie de la Sainte Famille. After she left Laurel Hill in 1916
Kate O'Brien did a BA degree in UCD. She is unusual among
Irish writers of her era in being both intellectual and from a

relatively privileged, although Catholic and nationalist, background. She herself described the profound intellectual influence on her of her French professor in UCD, Roger Chauviré
– how intellectual maturity was forced on her by his lectures.
(It is ironic, then, that some of her novels were regarded by
[mainly male] critics as 'noveletish'.) For most of her life Kate
O'Brien earned her living as a journalist, although she did
teach for some months in 1921 in St Mary's Girls' College in
Hampstead in London. Then, like Mary Lavelle in her novel of
that name, she went to the north of Spain as an au pair. She
was a reviewer for the *Manchester Guardian* and *The Times* and
had some financial success early in her career with the production of a play, *Distinguished Villa* (1926). In the 1960s she lived
in Roundstone in Co. Galway but returned to settle near
Faversham in Kent from 1970 until her death in 1974.

Within a decade of her death two of Kate O'Brien's best
novels, *The Ante-Room* and *The Land of Spices*, were reissued by
the Dublin-based feminist imprint Arlen House under the direction of Catherine Rose, in 1980 and 1982 respectively. Later
these titles passed to the feminist imprint Virago in London,
which in its Modern Classics series has republished neglected
women writers like Antonia White, Rosamund Lehmann and
Vita Sackville-West. Virago reissued *Mary Lavelle* (1984),
Without My Cloak (1986), *The Land of Spices* (1988), *The Ante-
Room* (1989) and *The Last of Summer* (1990) and have kept
these titles in print since then. The Virago Travellers series also
reissued O'Brien's interesting 1937 memoir-travelogue, *Farewell Spain*, in 1985, and this is now available again from House
of Stratus, a reprint publisher.

It seems likely, however, that the revival of interest in Kate
O'Brien was due in large part to two strokes of good fortune –

the establishment of feminist publishing houses and the development of a feminist literary discourse in Irish universities. This academic framework views O'Brien not just as a feminist writer in the sense that her heroines are women as independent as they can be in the society in which they live but as a lesbian novelist (a claim that has been denied by members of O'Brien's extended family in Limerick). For example, *Ordinary People Dancing*, a collection of critical essays on O'Brien published by Cork University Press in 1993, laments the inadequacies of two earlier critical monographs and attempts to reclaim the novelist for the Irish literary canon.[6] In his introduction the editor, Eibhear Walsh, rejects Procrustean feminist criticism:

> In many ways this unqualified championing and reclaiming of O'Brien as successful proto-feminist and victorious, uncomplicated radical is as counterproductive as outright neglect.[7]

However, most of the essays in the collection are by women academics and some might be seen to fall into the very category he takes care to eschew. In her essay entitled 'Out of Order: Kate O'Brien's lesbian fictions' Emma Donoghue is typically forthright:

> Reading Kate O'Brien as a lesbian novelist is as fruitful and as necessary, I suggest, as reading Elizabeth Bowen as Irish, Jane Austen as middle-class, or Alice Walker as black. But because 'lesbian' is more easily denied and avoided than these other labels, even in the 1990s, such overdue work on Kate O'Brien has not been done.[8]

(Naturally it was this essay that captured media attention and provided newspaper headlines when the book was published.)

Lesbian or not, it still seems to me that Kate O'Brien has

not received the critical attention or readership she deserves simply as a novelist. It was Joseph Conrad who described Henry James as a 'historian of fine conscience' and in *The Ante-Room* (1936) and *The Land of Spices* (1941), Kate O'Brien produced two works that might aptly be subtitled 'the portrait of a lady'. *The Ante-Room*, O'Brien's own favourite novel, is set in 1880, and impresses the reader as being consciously Jamesian. Indeed at one of the two dinner scenes which provide both the finest writing and the subtlest characterisation of the novel, the characters discuss James' *Washington Square*, which in 1880 was being serialised in *Cornell's Magazine*. As in all Kate O'Brien's novels the theme of forbidden love is central: in this case the intense attraction between the heroine Agnes Mulqueen and her brother-in-law Vincent. Agnes is Catholic, and fully aware of the sinfulness of her passion for Vincent. On the first of the three days of the novel's time-span, she goes to confession; on the second night she returns Vincent's passionate kiss in the summerhouse. It proves impossible for her to be implicitly faithful to her deeply-held Catholicism but neither is she morally blind. Although the intellectual in her is developed to a greater extent than the sensual and 'the love of his [Vincent's] touch' surprises her, latent sexual passion is suggested by her figure, even though it is the opposite of voluptuous (her thinness is emphasised in the novel) and by the style of her clothes. Where her sister, Marie Rose, is girlishly exquisite in white and pink frills, Agnes wears a tight-fitting sealskin jacket to go to church and a handsome, womanly black velvet dress that is noticed by the family's distinguished visitors at the second dinner party. As long as the novel focuses on Agnes, her bourgeois family life, her sense of duty and her relationship with the second man in the novel who loves and kisses her (and appreciates her true quality), William Curran, it is very fine indeed. Where it falters is in the dénouement. What is the solution to the insoluble dilemma of forbidden love? In this case, Vincent's suicide on the final pages. Perhaps it was flaws such as the ending of this novel that drew from critics the accusation that O'Brien was a 'noveletish' writer.

The Land of Spices (1941) is to my mind a better novel than *The Ante-Room*. Among its achievements is the sustained depiction of the moral and spiritual development of Helen Archer, the reverend mother of the Sainte Famille convent and school in Limerick in which almost all the action is set. The novel became infamous when it was banned in Ireland by the over-zealous Censorship of Publications Board for the phrase 'the embrace of love' – love between two men, Helen's father and his pupil, Etienne (although Seán Ó Faoláin mischievously suggested that the title itself outraged the censors, conveying to them the idea of spicy sex scenes rather than the poem by George Herbert, 'Prayer' from which it is taken):[9]

Her father's study was at the back of the house, above the kitchen. It had a long, wide balcony of wrought iron which ran full across the wall and ended in an iron staircase to the garden. This balcony made a pleasant, deep shade over the flagged space by the kitchen door, where Marie-Jeanne often sat to prepare vegetables, or to have a sleep...

Helen glanced in at the empty kitchen, scratched the cat behind the ears, and hoped that Marie-Jeanne wasn't getting too drunk at Malines. Then she ran up the iron stairs and along the balcony to the open window of her father's study.

She looked into the room.

Two people were there. But neither saw her; neither felt her shadow as it froze across the sun.

> She turned and descended the stairs. She left the garden and
> went on down the curve of Rue Saint Isidore.
>
> She had no objective and no knowledge of what she was
> doing. She did not see external things. She saw Etienne and her
> father, in the embrace of love.[10]

In the novel what is of interest is not the homosexual relationship itself but the effect on the teenage Helen, intelligent
and cultured but morally innocent, of the realisation of her
father's homosexuality. The shock exiles her from the paradise
of her father's devoted love and care and from the happiness of
her idyllic girlhood in Brussels. She gains knowledge – an
understanding of her late mother's unhappiness and of why her
father's academic career has taken place in exile from university life in England – but the knowledge is an unbearable
burden which she cannot share with a living soul, least of all
with her father. Furthermore it is knowledge without understanding or compassion because at this point Helen rejects all
human love. The experience has a cataclysmic effect on her
choice of career or vocation and on her subsequent life as a
nun, a teacher and a leader of others. The term most often used
of her by the uncomprehending Irish among whom she lives for
many years is 'cold': the 'cold, calm Reverend Mother'. Father
Conroy, the nationalist-leaning curate, thinks of her as 'a cold
English fish'. Mother Mary Andrew, an Irish revivalist who
comes from Co. Tyrone is equally hostile, and the bishop, more
urbane and pragmatic than either of these, sees her as a worthy
adversary, devoted to '*la pudeur et la politesse*', the mission of her
order, and out of step with the new Ireland which aspires as
soon as possible to jettison everything associated with the
colonial oppressor. (One of O'Brien's little-observed strengths

as a cultural commentator is that in a book dated September 1940 she pinpoints the tendency of Irish society – which certainly grew more pronounced as the century progressed, and reached its apogee with the Celtic Tiger culture of the 1990s – to throw the baby out with the bathwater.)

The lesson Helen Archer has to learn in the course of the novel is to soften her 'hard heart, that's bound up, and asleep'.[11] The character with whom she is paralleled, the young Anna Murphy, symbolises vulnerability and innocence when she recites Herbert's 'Peace' and seems to speak to Helen directly in one of her darkest moments. The effect the poem has on her derives from the fact that her father was a devoted and gifted scholar of the metaphysical poets, but also from the metaphysical reality that, whatever Helen's own judgement, her father may also be innocent in the sight of God. When Helen reads her father's last letter to her, she is conscious of this innocence, although for her it exists too as what she earlier calls naïveté, that is an ignorance of the reason for the profound change that had come over her when she was eighteen: 'She felt so peaceful in that realisation that she smiled, as often in girlhood she had done over his letters, at their characteristic ease and innocence. Innocence – to the very end – of all the woe and pain that lay between them.' (p.164) The *bonne à tout faire* (housekeeper), Marie-Jeanne, no intellectual, in the accompanying letter describes Henry Archer on his deathbed as '*Doux come un ange, mon grand pauvre – comme tu sais, chérie, comme toujours.*' (p.136) Although Marie-Jeanne's traditional Catholic mind is saddened by Archer's refusal of the sacraments she realises: '*et certes en ce qui le concerne, je ne dois pas avoir de soucis. Soit sûre que le bon Dieu connaît un saint.*' (p.136) There can be little that is more moving, more evocative of tenderness in modern Irish literature than these two letters, Marie Jeanne's rendered only in French.

Henry Archer may have been ignorant of the reason for Helen's turning away from his love but he sees very clearly its effect. On her return from Kracow to Brussels, where she spent some years before being sent to Ireland, he describes her to herself as 'lonely and merciless' (p.28), and despite all that she knows in an intellectual way of the love of God, her journey from inhumanity to a kind of humanity, from judgement to a degree of acceptance, is a long and painful one.

It is easy to see *The Land of Spices* as a feminist novel; only as a nun could Helen Archer achieve such a degree of authority and independence (the Sainte Famille, a foreign order, is independent even of the local bishop) in the first decades of the twentieth century. When the action of the novel ends, in 1914, it is against a backdrop of a continent that is about to change forever. Helen is on the point of returning to Brussels to take up overall leadership of the community. Like the young Kate O'Brien at roughly the same period, Anna Murphy has set her sights on higher education but the too-obvious clash between reverend mother and Anna's worldly grandmother, Mrs Condon, near the end of the novel seems to me to be an aesthetic failure, as do the perfunctory inclusion of the suffragette, Miss Robertson, and the paedophile judge, Mr Lawson, in the scenes set in the west of Ireland. But, as the introductory remark by Eibhear Walsh quoted earlier suggests, it may indeed be 'counterproductive' if not quite as 'counterproductive as neglect' to read a novel so full of beauty of thought and language as a feminist tract.[12]

Stand and Give Challenge:
Francis MacManus' *Flow On, Lovely River*

Although Kate O'Brien became an unbeliever while still in
school, there are many ways in which she qualifies as a 'Catholic' writer. Not for her the predictable literary route of denunci-
ation, the charting of loss of faith, of bitterness and anti-cleri-
calism. In her best novels her characters are Catholics trying to
reconcile human feeling and spiritual yearning. Francis Mac-
Manus wrote about Catholicism from the inside, as a believer;
in his fiction he challenged both Irish society and the Church
but abandoned neither the religion nor the country. Hence the
title 'Stand and Give Challenge' for a consideration of one of
his modern novels, *Flow on, Lovely River* (1941), the story of a
schoolmaster, John Lee. In an Ireland where Catholic doctrine
and morality has lost its influence with extraordinary speed and
where the concept of renunciation is now unthinkable, the
caveat expressed by Sean McMahon in his 1970 article on
MacManus is more relevant than ever:

> Perhaps here one should remind the reader that MacManus was a
> Catholic, as were most of his characters. This did not mean that
> they were pious or better than another but that their actions were
> consciously or unconsciously measured against certain exacting
> standards. They were precluded from certain courses, or took
> them with trembling and resultant remorse. Renunciation was not
> the alien idea it has become in other literatures. The Irish still re-
> garded their religion as the great important thing in their lives,
> whether they rejected it or impaled themselves upon it.[13]

Francis MacManus was born in Kilkenny city and that city and
its rural or small-town hinterland and the river that flows
through them are the setting for all his modern novels. He was

educated at St Patrick's College Drumcondra (where he must have been a contemporary of Bryan MacMahon) and UCD, and taught in Synge Street CBS in Dublin from 1930 until 1948, when he took up the newly-created position of head of talks and features at Radio Éireann. His novels include a historical trilogy, his first published works: *Stand and Give Challenge* (1934); *Candle for the Proud* (1936) and *Men Withering* (1939). These concern the life of the Gaelic poet Donncha Rua Mac Conmara (1715–1810), of whom MacManus writes in the foreword to *Stand and Give Challenge*: 'You and I, had we been alive and Irish and troubled with song, might have been such a person as the chief character who lived when a dark nightmare was on this nation.' Some might say that the puritanical Church-dominated Ireland of the 1930s was itself 'a dark nightmare' but MacManus is making precisely the point that public piety and lack of artistic freedom do not compare as miseries with the sufferings of the people of Gaelic Ireland in the penal era. His use of the word 'nation' is significant, since he was, I believe, a nationalist with a love of country, of his native place and of his own people of Kilkenny. This does not mean that he is a sentimental or soft-centred novelist; perhaps no other Irish writer of the twentieth century was as rigorous and tough as he, both in style and in content.

Flow on, Lovely River was published by Talbot Press in Dublin in 1941, the same year *The Land of Spices* appeared from William Heinemann in London. The two novels could hardly be more different, the first male and lapidary (despite its title), the second graceful and feminine, although both deal with schools and with the fate of teachers. *Flow on, Lovely River* was MacManus' first modern novel and the first of a trilogy set in and around Drombridge, a fictional Co. Kilkenny small town

within easy reach of the larger metropolis – it might be Ben-
nettsbridge or Thomastown; the others are *Watergate* (1942)
and *The Fire in the Dust* (1950). The title of the first comes
from a nineteenth-century sentimental ballad about doomed
love set against the backdrop of the River Suir:

> How sweet 'tis to roam by the sunny Suir stream
> And hear the doves coo neath the morning's sunbeam
> Where the thrush and the robin their sweet notes combine
> On the banks of the Suir that flows down by Mooncoin.
>
> *Chorus*
> Flow on, lovely river, flow gently along
> By your waters so sweet sounds the lark's merry song
> On your green banks I'll wander where first I did join
> With you, lovely Molly, the Rose of Mooncoin.

MacManus' river in this novel and elsewhere is the Suir's
equally lovely sister, the Nore. His aesthetic technique is to
portray the unvarnished reality of Irish life in the 1930s and
1940s by concentrating intensely on the interior life of his
protagonist. *Flow On, Lovely River* is a fine portrayal of the life
of a primary schoolteacher, John Lee, with all its frustrations –
the petty oppressions of priest and inspector, the soulless
pedagogy, the isolation, the lack of collegiality, the hypocritical
judgements of the small-townspeople, the protagonist's own
loss of promise (Lee refers to 'this old church without which I
have been promising myself to write a little history for a long
and fruitless time' [p.19]). It consists entirely of the journal of
John Lee, rendered in a spare and laconic style. There is no
need for an authorial voice to question the protagonist's
account of events or his understanding – Lee himself is given

the task of judge and unrelenting critic. Even in a town where he is little liked, where he is subject to abuses of authority by Church and State, he has no harsher critic than himself. Benedict Kiely wrote of MacManus' style: 'His sentences are always hard, like bricks built round a tomb, never soft like the sweep of a garment round the graceful body.'[14] This may be true when the novelist is describing the heartless publican, the venal sergeant, the authoritarian priest or Lee's own inadequacies – but it is not universal. Only when he is observing the River Nore does John Lee allow himself a true consciousness of beauty. And his creator has these words to describe it:

> Where the mill stream fans out under willows and deepens till the drowned weeds are only dark stains on the gravel, I turned left and went up by the Nore. The light had dribbled then to a corner of the sky, and the loveliest of rivers was like glass flushed faintly, in which the reeds, the sky, the willows and even a sloping field of wheat-stooks swayed gently, a rosy lost world that a few scudding swallows pretended to reach by diving among the swarms of midges. When I came to sit on the parapet of Garvan Bridge I felt as still and receptive as the slow waters, and I stayed there, moodless, to watch the inverted bowl of the firmament fill up with darkness and a few stars, moving like golden stars, far below. (pp.7–8)[15]

It is at Garvan Bridge that Lee first meets Kit Hennessy, and the river is a symbol of their love, of life itself, away from the petty restrictions of Lee's respectable position. In his later imaginings, 'She walks and talks and the Nore runs smoothly behind us' (p.25). But the Nore is also a symbol of isolation, of indifference. Father Joe Walsh, the curate, more charitable by far than Father Rice, the parish priest and 'spiritual sergeant major', as Father Joe describes him, says of Kit's father, Vimy Hennessy:

Hennessy, John, is like the most of us, like that river out there, flowing on and on, never knowing anything long enough, until it reaches the sea (p.19).

Kit Hennessy is the daughter of a drunken reprobate, and her sisters have earned the opprobrium of the town's moral arbiters, such as Lee's housekeeper, Mrs Byrne, for leading young men astray: 'two good-for-nothing fly-by-nights of daughters' (p.22). Even Father Joe, the charitable curate and the nearest John Lee has to a friend, sees his infatuation with Kit as being disastrous and encourages him to marry the young woman with whom he has half-heartedly been keeping company, Statia Lennon. In September, when the action of the novel begins, Lee is isolated:

> No one replied [to his 'Goodnight']. I still had their silence with me as I ate my supper and turned up the lamp to write this, and read for a bit (p.10).

As the scholastic year – the teacher's year – unfolds, as the days darken and shorten, so his life darkens, his isolation increases. Although it is spring when the action of the novel ends and there is a hint of warmth, it is mainly the cold of the previous chapters that one remembers.

John Lee might be expected to marry Statia out of inertia or force of habit but he knows that he will never do so. In the creation of the Lennon family here and in *Watergate*, Mac-Manus' version of rural Ireland is not of impoverished peasants but of solid, prosperous farmers. But Lee's taste runs to the thin, impoverished, mysterious and romantic-seeming Kit rather than to hearty, sensual Statia:

There's no decay in the Lennons; and there can't have been any decay for generations. Busily, they try to make themselves comfortable, decent, well-behaved; and yet, liveliness breaks out on them like warts. Now, my own mother, God rest her, must have given me this inward turn of mind from which I often recoil like a released, overwound spring. She seldom rose to meet hardship and trials and to fight them desperately. Instead, she bowed her head, said her prayers, brooded, and let the wave pass over her; and oddly enough, things nearly always came right. It's another way of surviving.

Kit, on the other hand, is elusive. She accepts John Lee's kiss (he is rarely shown bestowing any sign of affection on Statia) without protest, but impassively, giving him no indication that she returns his affection. After meeting her by the river he is driven by frustration to compare her effect on him to its ceaseless Heraclitean flow: 'My body seems to respond to the movement of the river once more, and it is movement that I cannot dam for one instant as it gathers momentum, charges through me, curves, drops, slides, races and foams out into the black leagues of the sea. Yes. She's like the river' (p.67). It becomes clear at their final meeting by the river towards the end of the novel that she valued him for his friendship in a hostile world; she is shocked by his proposal of marriage.

John Lee persists in his courtship of Kit Hennessy despite universal disapproval and the real threat of losing his job because of the opposition of Father Rice. Before spring comes to Drombridge he loses Kit, the woman he loves (she chooses the peace of a convent in Dublin, which she enters as a lay sister) but because of the sudden death of Father Rice he is spared the ignominious dismissal that the parish priest had intended for him – a dismissal coupled with a good reference, as was often the custom of the time. Despite the authoritarianism of Father Rice, the novel is not anti-clerical. The parish priest is no raging demagogue but paternal, patient, himself worn out by the strains of his office. Statia, too, refuses to abandon Lee. She is not blind to his infatuation for Kit Hennessy but like the other woman she values his friendship. She is like her family, so much admired by the outsider John Lee, not least for their capacity for humour.

It is in reality John Lee's misfortune to be allowed to remain in his position in Drombridge, returned to educational drudgery at the end of the novel. It seems likely, despite Statia's forbearance, that he will never love again, that he will remain a bachelor. In MacManus' next novel, *Watergate*, which is narrated by Peter Walsh, a cousin of the Lennon family, Lee makes a brief appearance in Shea's bar:

> Then he hid his thin Spanish monk's face behind a newspaper … Shea placed a glass of beer beside him, and he sipped it indifferently, as through habit. Although he had been a close family friend of the Lennons once, visiting the house almost every second night so that they had come to know him fairly well and to like him in a reserved way, yet there was a coolness between them now, chiefly because it had seemed at one time that he would marry Statia Lennon.[16]

Bryan MacMahon and Francis MacManus have both provided portraits of the life of a primary schoolteacher in small-town Ireland in the early and middle decades of the twentieth century but the mindset represented in these books is a world apart. MacMahon's book *The Master* is all of a piece in its outlook, although the teaching life may not be a bed of roses. He is both specific and general in the accounts he gives of his pedagogy, and of the philosophy underpinning it:

> I do not think that it is a part of the teacher's duty to convey to
> the children the false notion that life is devoid of malice, injury,
> ill-fortune, treachery or injustice ... But somehow or other he
> should never cease to promote in children the determination to
> say 'Yes' to life, to the dark as well as to the bright of it, to its
> beauty and glory, to its lapses from grace into degradation and its
> eventual restoration to serenity. (p.90)

For schoolmaster John Lee it is a more basic question of his
own survival in a harsh, unforgiving society. To paraphrase his
own description of his mother: the hopelessly compromised
half-life that is left to him at the end of the novel is 'another
way of surviving' (p.33). He lacks the sense of community that
is so evident in *The Master*; the curiosity about his fellow-man;
and the intellectual interests – or rather the will to pursue
them. Above all he lacks the creativity enjoyed by MacMahon
that opens the shutter of 'the camera of the human eye' (p.105)
and transforms everything observed into story.

1 Except for a term which he spent in Iowa, USA, in 1963.
2 Published in Dublin by Talbot Press, 1973.
3 *Patsy-O* (1989) and *Mascot Patsy-O* (1992).
4 Gabriel Fitzmaurice, 'The Gift of Ink: the Passing of the Storyman'
    in *Kerry on My Mind: of Poets, Pedagogues and Place* (Clare:
    Salmon Publishing, 1999).
5 This reference is to the Poolbeg paperback edition (1993), p. 65.
    Further references to this edition are given in parenthesis.
6 Laura Reynolds, *Kate O'Brien: a Literary Portrait* (Gerrards Cross:
    Colin Smythe, 1987); and Adèle Dalsimer, *Kate O'Brien: A Criti-
    cal Study* (Dublin: Gill and Macmillan, 1990).

7 Eibhear Walsh (ed.), *Ordinary People Dancing* (Cork: Cork University Press, 1993), p. 1.

8 Emma Donoghue, 'Out of Order: Kate O'Brien's Lesbian Fictions' in Eibhear Walsh (ed.), *Ordinary People Dancing*, pp. 36–7.

9 'The milkie way, the bird of Paradise,
  Church-bells beyond the stares heard, the souls bloud,
  The land of spices; something understood.'

  – George Herbert (1593–1633), 'Prayer'

10 This reference is to the Arlen House edition of *The Land of Spices* (1982), p. 157. Further references to this edition are given in parenthesis.

11 Yet, if as thou doest melt, and with they traine
  Of drops make soft the Earth, my eyes could weep
  O'er my hard heart, that's bound up and asleep.
    Perhaps at last
    Some such showres past,
  My God would give a Sunshine after raine.

  – Henry Vaughan (1621–1695), 'The Showre'

12 See note 4 above.

13 Sean McMahon, 'Francis MacManus' Novels of Modern Ireland' in *Éire-Ireland*, 1970.

14 *The Kilkenny Magazine*, No. 14 (Spring–Summer), 1966, p. 127.

15 This reference is to the Mercier paperback edition of *Flow On, Lovely River* (1966), p. 16. Further references to this edition are given in parenthesis.

16 *Watergate* (Dublin: Talbot Press, 1941), p. 51.

CHAPTER FOUR

The World of Story

Suzanne Brown

The world of story is our world. Real life characters are a perpetual source of interest to human beings. Almost everyone talks about people they encounter, and the fabric of little incidents that happen to them. They might tell how a cranky neighbour chased some children away after their football had marked her sheets, only to find on her return that her dog had pulled one off the line, or they might relate how a kind postmistress had noticed they were paying a hospital fee and asked what was wrong. In each little story cameo portraits are created. The feeling of a place's rhythm and pace comes to life. In Bryan MacMahon's non-fictional prose (such as *The Master* and *The Storyman*) these come together to give a whole sense of life. Life full of pattern and emotion flows onward, as characters create their world. Their village is what they make it, by their work, their pattern of politics, their cultural enthusiasms. They light up the pages, just as they light up our lives.

But this sense of life can also be suddenly illuminated by a striking event so deeply characteristic of the thrust and inner development of people's lives as to be an even more startling and profound expression of their feelings. Of these watershed events MacMahon makes short-stories. Think of the story 'The

Miler' in *The Sound of Hooves*. A girl too alive for the humdrum is self-disciplined enough to keep a bed and breakfast and survive. Yet a moment of her passion breaks through. Passion washes over her and her young visitor, changes the breadth and colour of their experience, and then subsides, having altered their world, which expands to contain it. For MacMahon the sense of communal life is strong enough to embrace the power of individual passion. Such a rich web of communal life makes for an emotionally rich story. The community, to be vibrant, allows for much individuality. A writer's own sense that life belongs to the brave emerges, and characters and community find their own balance. Sometimes a character defeated by his timidity in the face of restrictions re-emerges, in time, to warn another. The community absorbs his warning, and life-denying defeats are made generous use of, so that the sense of what can rightly be done is enriched for the next generation. Erosion of restriction is one of his themes. Think of the story 'The Sound of Hooves' in which the old harnessmaker warms to the subject of his missed love to alert a would-be priest about the poverty he sees in a cold celibacy.

Another theme explored is the danger of anger in that it makes a frozen caricature of another life despite the fact that that life is ongoing and self-renewing. MacMahon portrays feuding quarrels and political turbulence with a deep sadness. For example, in 'The Storyman' a grieving son turns to a local radio-station man and asks him never to play a ballad in which his father appears in a murky light: 'Forget that bloody ould ballad, will you!'

MacMahon believes the native energies of old Irish culture are irrepressible and utterly worthwhile. He was a schoolmaster who spent his evenings in sessions of music and talk: this was the real treasure grown out of the ground, the food, real as potatoes, to nourish his pupils as well as himself. The feel of Ireland's weather is in this music, in the legends is told the play of shadow and sunlight, the pace of the bright rivers and mountain streams are repeated in conversation's flow. What comes from outside can be absorbed, but it will be changed in the mix. What a poem means to a nine year old from Kerry comes partly from what the child brings to it. Sometimes in his description of schoolchildren in *The Master* MacMahon's anger and frustration at what impedes their growth comes through. Yet this is rooted in a faith that there is a right growth, a way they would uniquely be if they received plenty of nourishment. Every teacher knows that children try to absorb what they need, like young plants, and discard the rest. MacMahon communicates a rich sense that they need to engage with what we as teachers offer, and to work with us to grow. He fears ignorance as he fears hunger, but he recognises that the children's knowledge comes not only from the classroom, but also from the community and the natural world, and that what the classroom offers them must be appropriate to the culture in which they live. Of himself as a child he says, 'At the back of my mind, I held fast to the notion that each experience, whether humorous, doleful or exalting or, indeed, a combination of all three attributes, would prove useful in the years ahead ... I was observing, closely observing ... My native town as a whole, all Ireland and beyond, had yet to be explored and savoured. And what I found was to be stored in the secret treasure-house of the subconscious.'

Learning can expand children's experience, but it must connect. It can challenge the norms they sense around them, even break and remake them, allowing the community to enfold new experiences but it must work with their sense of belonging.

Even when they go away, they find they need to stay rooted to home. They adventure away, partly to bring the tale home. And the tale is meant to be shared, seen reflected in the eyes of the listeners, as it winds on. People are communal, the sharing benefits both the teller and the listener. The exotic is to be wondered at, compared and related to, but always from the sense of who one is and where roots plunge deepest. Then real growth, and real learning, happen.

In another mood, MacMahon emphasises that the problems faced at home come with one everywhere; both the troubles and the joys of home are carried in the heart. This is a universal human experience, especially for emigrants, who try to cope with a barrage of new situations. Sometimes it is very hard, but with the sorrow comes the song. The scene of drunken Irishmen singing ballads as the Kentucky sun rises moves all. We sense again how we long to recreate the place, the hills, the weather, the village or neighbourhood we came from to give it eternal life. The artistic urge is partly this. Richard Murphy once said 'Loss is the mother of memory', and when Seamus Heaney was asked if his poems were often elegies, he said, 'what else would they be?' Even Shakespeare said in a surge of hope, 'As long as this lives, this gives life to thee'.

This too is part of the teaching urge. Who has not felt a thrill on offering an old legend from one's own area, or when explaining a hill fort or when allowing an old text to give voice to a human experience that happened two thousand years ago? The richest sense of heritage imbues them all with its sunset flames.

So supporting that hold on communal life is the theme I will deal with in this chapter. In the spirit of Bryan MacMahon, I want to talk about ways to enrich children's deep sense of belonging to the special culture of their area.

Every school has a catchment area that potentially is a community. When I work in country schools, I find the natural world bears the human traces of a thousand stories. Children love learning those stories associated with place names and re-creating scenes from mythic events outside. They love following old trackways and making maps of how their area looked in previous centuries.

They also create a story world of the present features. On my north Dublin street is a stone wall with a hidey-hole for messages and beyond the wall is a cemetary for washed-up sailors, each a ghostly presence. But the twelfth-century church spreads its deep rooted and sunny peace like an old tree. It is on the site of an earlier beehive hermit's cell – surely a friend of St Kevin's. Why the hermit came to this coastal area miles from Glendalough is a story that only the wind knows. But for older children a clue is that the site had earlier been a pre-Christian holy place, and that the full moon ribbons light across Dublin Bay in full view of his hut, linking Dalkey and Howth by a path of light. Nearby are dolmens and a fairy ring in the grounds of a Norman castle occasionally visited (even now?) by the ghost of Grace O'Malley the pirate. A medieval walkway from Dublin city to Howth can still be faintly traced in a footpath right of way behind my house and the others on the street. Giving children a chance to map all this on a sheet where no modern houses are marked offers a welter of imaginative free play after school and in long summer days.

Children in Ballymun flats similar to those of dreary industrial towns trace their place back to the early middle ages and to saints scarcely known now, but mentioned in local churches. Along the open cavern that is the stairwell of one towerblock is an incredibly alive picture of a brown horse. Under it is writ-

ten: 'I will never leave you.' Horses graze in the grass outside
and a hot debate is whether the new sheltered paddock is free
enough for such beings to winter in.

A further two miles down the coast near me are smugglers'
caves which have been used even in the twentieth century and
for how long before? Trees in their thousands forested the hills
when Finn's men roamed from here to Kildare. Their tree-lore,
wood-lore, coastal knowledge, their campfire stories about adventures, their tales of the Fianna, can all be rooted into the
children's love of their area. Even then, a fire burned on Howth
Hill to warn ships of rocks and danger. Shipwreck stories are a
natural ooh-aah source of wonder. Nowhere in Ireland is far
from the sea and caves and old lighthouses are easily located.

Setting tales in the children's own area fills their imagi-
nations with a love of the place. They will easily create other
stories, poems, songs and wonderful artwork, as a natural fol-
low-on. And of course you hope you are enriching their private
imaginary-playtime with friends after school.

Sometimes the flow can work in the other direction. Children can choose, and illustrate, spots near home, and then relate made-up stories about, for example, the gnarled tree (perhaps treasure was buried in its roots), the old empty house in a
field (who hid there?), etc. Simple artefacts, a leather satchel,
a piece of jewellery or a coin, can spur the story on. Preparatory
work can include drawing the scene day and night, or stormy
and fair weather.

Very young children (infant classes) often like to begin by
mapping the landscape of a loved picture-book story, making
one map per table of four pupils. I did this recently with *Katie
Morag Delivers the Mail*: on one side of the map they worked
together to draw the island and the other side had Grandma

Island's farm. Gradually we added details, and small clothespeg people to be the characters. These playmats can then start off other stories about the same characters. Young children love making weather sounds, and animal sounds, so the final telling of any story can be shared in a very dramatic way. The playmats and figures can become part of the story-corner, pulled out in free play periods.

Most public libraries will help with local history material. Many hold events in conjunction with local history groups where a member can come to share local history with the older children. They enjoy building up projects which include research and story. The living presence of history enormously enriches life and this is as true of parts of Dublin, Cork or Galway, as it is of more remote country areas. Local landmarks, monasteries, wells, harbours, castles, all provide a wealth of settings. Time travel is an easy concept for eight to twelve year olds to play with. An hour of serious preparation choosing names, grouping in families, thinking about occupations and dwellings, and writing up notes on characters' personal histories, turns nine year olds into fully fledged Vikings or Celts. Then details of being a blacksmith, or a weaver or a potter, become urgently needed. Attempts at craft are made: designing plaids, doing simple weaving, grinding grain between two stones, making bits of dress-up clothing and jewellery. Moreover, as each child chooses their family and the tables become homes and workplaces, a community is born. A little story about the family can then be written in the voice of a family member. For most children this family will also include wonderful animals – loving horses, faithful dogs. Each family has its role in the village and its special burdens and needs. You the teacher, as wandering craftsman or druid, can visit the village, and warn of a sudden danger. Roleplaying sessions build, an hour or two each week, to create magical alternative lives, with projects like tree-naming, or practice-weaving, in between. Rune or ogham can be used to create special objects.

A second class imagining being Celts made a wonderful tree book, with leaves and buds of about thirty species, carefully named in Irish and English and, where known, in the old Druidic ogham letter associated with the tree. Details of a tree's special traditional uses, e.g. hazel for dousing rods, sallow leaves for pain relief, birch for making fine paper or a light beverage, were talked about; so was folklore about the green birch-lady, and the magical rowan berries. Many curriculum areas were touched on. As we roleplayed a journey to Tara, decisions had to be made each campfire time, based on what the lookouts had seen. We were watching especially for Picts whose strange ships had been spotted off the coast. We and other villages were to assemble at Tara, working out whether to welcome the strangers or to fight them. A storm, or a broken wagon wheel could halt us, but we kept our spirits up with old eerie tales. Grave decisions involved the horse-whisperer speaking to one of our magical old horses and asking him for guidance. In the end they and the angels protected us and we safely met some Picts and made new friendships. The Picts were sea-rovers from Scotland, so new tales could be heard. We were a forged community, we had adventured together, helping one another.

Also, as Celtic children, some of them had made pine twig-people dolls which could be brought home, along with clay pots, tweed capes, etc. They remind of the adventure and stimulate further play. With the roleplaying teacher asking questions or spotting possibilities, the children created their story over four or five sessions. The sense of being one with the Celts runs very deep. This work is a cross between drama and story, perhaps best described as 'living story'. This kind of work is unforgettable and very rewarding. The adult feels lucky to be joining in genuine play with the children making or imagining everything they bring.

Twig people featured in another class as secret dwellers in a nearby forest, with a world of their own, and tales to tell. They can talk to birds and squirrels who of course live very different lives. Some have come to live in the senior infants' story corner, in a couple of paper trees, where free play can happen on rainy days.

Finger puppets and sock puppets can also turn into villagers for a third or fourth class. Each puppet has his or her own quirky character and lives in a cardboard house (made in art sessions). Once a week, these can be grouped into a village and a story can be started. I found after two goes that the children made up their own stories. All of this re-instills the habit of real imaginative effort, and a skill in toy-making is useful in our low-budget future. The detail of what they made amazed me. This group was setting stories in about 1700. Each sock puppet lived in a family except for the weaver who lived under the magical tree and wove baby blankets out of sunset. If time allows, each table can prepare one story that features their family, so a *Canterbury Tales* kind of structure holds it all together. In our first story a widower's daughter set off from table to table, asking for help for her ailing father, and eventually making her way into the magic forest at the centre. A puppet with such a deep character lives forever, her experiences only enrich her personality. Emotional quandaries can be explored, fears overcome (e.g. of the two deaf elderly spinsters reputed to be witches). Fears of boating can be helped by a kindly young boatman, and who knows what will come of that friendship in the long run? Puppets' lives go on while the children are away doing other things.

Family patterns vary greatly in such a village, so the children's sense of the many kinds of lives in their own community heightens. A lot of group work creates mini-communities in class, too. Building a bridge from one table to another, or working out how to set up a forest together, are worthwhile for the sharing of effort and ideas. Using simple materials and lots of tape, children can make just about anything and a gap of a day or two means lots of fresh material turns up from home and outside. Song and musical effects are great to add in and are, of course, free. So the children easily turn the classroom into an imagined puppets' village. A few cut branches propped in styrofoam become a forest. Cardboard houses sprout up on tables. Blue cloth is a river, and near to it, firebirds hatch out of gold yarn nests and swarm, spreading golden magic. The little characters come to life, and a teacher acting as a narrator, with perhaps a puppet on her hand, can weave their ideas together, providing each group with a scene, and letting spontaneous decisions lead the story on. This way of working is close to the way children play and allows each to create. Rather than a script, you need an earlier session to get to know the characters the children are imagining, and a sense of what situations would involve those characters in meaningful decisions.

Older children also love being characters in a roleplay. One class of ten year olds decided they would be archaeologists and anthropologists sent out by a geographical society to explore lost cities. One of the speakers at the opening meeting was a teenager whom FÁS had sent out on a dig, in real life, and she gave them valuable advice. At the society's 'meeting' the teacher offered possible assignments such as exploring ruins in Peru, searching for a lost city in a Zimbabwean jungle, and visiting a Maori tribal settlement in New Zealand. Other children planned to climb the Himalayas, taping Sherpa music and dance, or getting geological samples from a Hawaiian volcano. At the meeting they planned equipment lists, chose different Swiss army knives, thought about safety equipment, and studied the terrain from maps and travel guidebooks. With the help of a wonderful book called *Outdoor Survival Skills* by Larry Olsen they worked out ways to survive when rivers flooded or hurricanes swept away the gear. They designed temporary shelters. Each group studied the travel guidebook for possible risks, thought about dangerous snakes, insects, or larger creatures, practised a bit of real first aid, took a deep breath, and set off.

Week by week, they searched wildlife magazines for photographs, raided libraries and internet for information, and made tapes to record their nightly journals. They filled in flora and fauna journals, and each 'specialist' wrote up notes to relay back on sites, tribal habits or plant and animal life. The teams bonded wonderfully. Artefacts were found, chips of pots were pieced together and odd bits of writing were translated. No one could use equipment forgotten or already lost. Food had to be scavenged if supplies were lost, so edible plants were studied. Cultural connections had to be made with native people, so their myths and music were dipped into. The whole experience was incredibly rich, and warm good fun. Geography and world cultures became real, wonderful and ready for exploring. Discussions about climate, shelter, crops and living patterns went on in a colourful living awareness. Patterns of communities were incredibly interesting and without even knowing it we had formed ways for these highly skilled photographers, biologists, archaeologists and mechanically gifted guides and radio people to work together.

Like the earlier story set in a Celtic village, the game integrated different kinds of lore, from geography to creation myths, from route-planning and mapping to quick sketches of plants and animals, from applications for grant money to emergency radio messages. It touched many curriculum areas, and brought knowledge that was needed. Children love learning what they feel they need to know. They love a sense of developing individual gifts to contribute to a common adventure. For a while the classroom was more like the larger adult world, with its many possible life-experiences for adults, its many callings, and ways of co-operating. As a teacher, I rewrote my lesson plans in the light of what they were doing, re-thought possible tasks over and over, turned to Trocaire's rich curriculum materials, to travel guides and history books and the indispensable *National Geographic* magazines, provided tapes, artefacts, music and watched them happily at work.

There are many other possibilities for this kind of curriculum-based study and adventure. Another class decided to be learned Egyptologists, who built clay and cardboard models of an Egyptian village with fishermen, basket weavers, clay pot makers, etc., made of plasticine and clay. They set up scenes and took photos to build up a book about these characters. They listened to legends and myths which they loved and then to 'wondertales' as Egyptians would have. They then pooled their own ideas to create a wondertale full of smuggling, dramatic changes in fortune, mythic maidens who shape-changed into winds, lost treasures and speaking beasts. One girl then wrote her own story, all in hieroglyphics. Others wrote personal histories for slaves, for pyramid builders and princes, etc. Again, the individual class' bent had to be respected; some were quieter craftmakers and book lovers, different to the explorers who fell down ravines and ice-crevasses. But a hum, a tone, emerges from a group after a while, and they work out their own preferred way to combine. This too is like adult life. It is one of the joys of teaching that few projects repeat in exactly the same way. A teacher watches what works, what the children settle to, and tries to create work that supports this and extends it. You listen, and search for what sparks activity and spontaneous contributing, what lights up their eyes and gets them bringing in extra bits, what kind of work starts that happy busy-ness. This can lead to assignments that are not graded, but appreciated, and tasks that are demanding but not competitive. It is open-ended and nourishes play and study outside of school, and maybe even a day dream or two. Along with our other teaching methods, it has a real place in primary, and hopefully in secondary, school.

There are three more kinds of work I want to look at which contribute to a deeper feel for the communal heartbeat of our towns, villages and city neighbourhoods. One has to do with making storybooks with junior cycle children. A young teacher described to me how her children had a forest corner in the senior infant class, with a large cardboard tree and a forest floor. Each child chose an animal they would love to be, e.g. a squirrel, rabbit, mouse, bear, woodpecker. Each found out about his/her animal's way of life, nocturnal or diurnal, hunter or hunted, leaf-eater or nut gatherer, lover of a burrow, a tree-hole, or an open sky. Every day they wove a story with a different child's animal as hero, then they created an anthology of their own, and turned it into a book.

Also for the very young, books about their toys' adventures are a real pleasure. Another young teacher introduced Sam, a class teddy, who went home with one child each day, and shared adventures with him. She sent an accompanying letter to the parents, explaining that this was a real outing for Sam, which could include family time and/or things like fighting dragons. She asked that the child make a picture of what they had done, to help them share it with the class the next morning. The next day, she acted as scribe for the adventure, and put the tale down at the bottom of the drawing. This became the book of Sam's adventures. As the year went on, the pictures became more complicated, sometimes three or four pictures would come in, and the stories became more and more exciting.

Many other wonderful books have come into the story-classes in the in-service fourth-year training. Tales from old sites in an area, or tales set along a nearby coast can be collected, made up and 'published' in a format full of maps, photos and artwork. All of these emphasise how landscape is an influence in all our lives, helping to create the kinds of adventures we have. Imagine working on different kinds of stories, a mystery set in eighteenth-century Cork, a lazy canal story set a hundred years ago, a packet of letters from a girl working as a maid in Dublin to her seaman brother, etc.

Circle-time is a natural place for sharing and creating stories. Teachers use many different styles, sometimes a story bag of old objects is passed round and each object tells its story, everything from 'I was a wooden spoon your mother was using to mix the Christmas stuffing when Santa came early ...' to 'I was a footprint left to fossilise by a mastadon hunted by stone age men near here ...' This is a method used by the National Museum's visiting storytellers and teacher-facilitators, who tour the country's classrooms with a suitcase full of unusual items, like a Chinese little red slipper or a replica Viking helmet. Some weekend sessions in Collins Barracks have a teller bringing in a few artefacts like a sword and a document to set off the stories. Another method, once the children are used to this, is giving groups the names of three of four objects they have to include in a tale they create together, e.g. a wooden raft, a binoculars, a feather and an arrow. Or a ticket, a broken watch, a subway map and an old key. They can tell these stories in campfire-style circle-time.

Another favourite project is writing stories as if they were sets of old letters found in an attic. This introduces the sense of voices from the past.

This kindly sense of the way old objects tell us human stories is being fostered, and surely this is part of why and how we learn to love history and museums.

Real voices from past childhoods were heard in a 1930s National Folklore Commission project, for which every primary school child in the country asked an elderly relative or neighbour to tell their favourite story from childhood, be it myth, ghost story, pirate tale or funny family story. These were collected and stored in St Patrick's in Drumcondra. This is an easy project to duplicate on a local scale. It involves the community at large in showing the children their heritage.

A rich variation on this is a recent project called 'Bridging the Gap', which the government have published a booklet to illustrate. It was designed by Carmel Maginn, a community school art teacher, in co-operation with a Dublin primary school. Eight elderly people were asked to tell about their lives; each story was unique and all were rewarding. One man, a recluse, turned out to be an inventor who had helped design the original computers, was still in touch with other inventors across the world, and was still working at eighty-three! Another described having the same best friend for seventy years and told of how warm and full their relationship had become. A third told a love story about a lost young soldier. A fourth described life in the flats during the Civil War. A fifth was a traveller who had many adventures. All the stories were interesting and vibrant, not at all about feeble old age. All of these people had been chosen at random to represent some part of a somewhat estranged elderly population, yet they came into the school and became real friends with the children who made art work and plays out of their stories. To help this along the local council offered two recent unemployed art college graduates the chance of a free exhibition in exchange for working with the children with the various art techniques. A young writer also helped with the play. The whole project cost little and has brought wonderful rewards to the area in a renewal of generations-friendships. Children have a natural affinity for grandparents, real and adopted.

In all of the projects I have been describing, I feel the same deep childhood urge to belong to a wider community. Some of the projects emphasise the people we live among, some the world of our past, some tell of the call of the natural world and the way it shapes our experience, some even tell of the animals around us, some of the ghosts of ancestors and the mythic sense of place. All this is our inheritance that we as teachers can impart and share – it's a two-way gift between the children and us. The heart belongs in its own landscape of the place, people and culture that nourish it and tries to give back, in teaching and writing, all it learns. MacMahon knew this and lived in this way. *The Master* throbs with the painful surge of life and shows MacMahon's rich appreciation of the children's lives both in and out of school. As teachers we sense the truth of what he writes. What greater fellowship can we feel for a writer than to go out and do what he tells us about? So leave the book and go enjoy teaching, and writing, and really nurturing children and, in turn, learning from them.

CHAPTER FIVE

The Ballad Tradition in North Kerry and West Limerick

Garry McMahon

Daniel Corkery, that wonderful receptacle and interpreter of the old Gaelic mentality as exemplified in the Munster poets of the eighteenth century, in his extraordinary book, *The Hidden Ireland*, is where I begin this chapter. It is my belief that our ballad tradition springs in a major way from the well of poetry which gushed forth from the pens of Eoghan Rua Ó Súilleabháin, Aogán Ó Rathaille, Brian Merriman and, to a lesser extent, Donnchadh Rua Mac Con Mara, Tadhg Gaelach Ó Súilleabháin (the man from Tournafulla), Sean Ó Tuama, Aindrias Mac Craith and others.

This of course was the age of the ascendancy (Gaelic and planter) which saw the gradual erosion of the Irish parliament culminating in the Act of Union at the beginning of the nineteenth century. The native Irish were looked down on by the English ascendancy as a lesser breed, and anything that was theirs therefore had to be inferior. This applied to their language and their song; the Gaelic poets who were entirely unknown to the planter ascendancy were really a hidden romantic literary underground. I would hold that these poets were, in large measure, the precursors of the ballad tradition which eventually survived, albeit in a changed state, to the present day. The English language, of course, replaced the Gaelic tongue in the eighteenth and nineteenth centuries.

The great Irish houses had welcomed poets, harpists and musicians and it is not too much of a leap of the imagination to visualise songs, poems and ballads being sung at banquets with or without accompaniment. Poets were rewarded for their verses and their singing. Songs of venom, and of praise too, came forth from their lips and their pens, causing them to be feared by their enemies as well as respected by their friends and patrons. I recall my late father, Bryan MacMahon, telling me of a person carrying a coffin who had been mentioned in a ballad tightening at the sight of the author of the song and suddenly blurting out: 'Wouldn't you forget that old ballad wouldn't you.'

The power of the ballad has lived on, even into the twentieth and the twenty-first centuries. In the nineteenth century as the English took over more and more in the field of the ballad, the broadside or broad sheet ballad (which I hold was largely an English invention) became more commonplace in Ireland. Ballot or ballad singers frequented fairs and patterns and these ballads, in English, were for the most part (at the beginning at least) certainly more Anglo than Irish in content although undoubtedly the influences were being cross fertilised from both sides. The ballad sheets of that time were the equivalent of the tape or CD of today. In England enormous quantities of the sheets were sold up and down the countryside and hundreds, if not thousands, were commonly disposed of at a single fair time.

Isaac Walton published his famous book, *The Compleat Angler*, in 1653 and in it after a day's fishing he speaks of enjoying 'An honest Ale-house where we shall find a cleanly room, lavender on the windows and twenty ballads stuck about the walls'.

The Napoleonic wars gave rise to a vast amount of ballads in the country, with songs in Napoleon's honour which are still sung to this very day – the Irish of course were very pro-Bonaparte. I think of the 'Bonny Bunch of Roses O' and 'My Bonny White Horseman' among others. Thomas Davis in *The Nation* newspaper published ballads which were eating and drinking to a beggar people. The vast majority of these could not read or write but the songs were read or sung to them by literate men desiring, no doubt, to imbue their listeners with the nationalistic fervor which filtered through the young Irelanders and the Fenians.

An English folksong collector, Alfred Williams, deserves mention here. He served in the British army in Ireland and was in this country in 1916. When he was subsequently demobbed in 1919, he went on a mission along the upper Thames valley visiting fairs, inns, markets and any place where he could inveigle singers to give him the words of country songs. Amazingly he collected up to four hundred ballads. These songs had to do with 'Ploughing, shearing, hunting, soldiering, poaching, harvesting, gypsying, highway robbers, drinking and wenching'. My father wrote an article about him romantically entitled 'The Auxie who loved ballads'.

There is no doubt these broad sheet ballads crossed the Irish Sea and became part of the Irish repertoire of ballads, cheek by jowl with the burgeoning ballad boom in English which had taken over from the Irish language songs in the second half of the nineteenth century. Local ballad makers began to compose songs to do with their own districts, events or people in their parishes, as distinct from the national songs painted on a broader canvas. North Kerry and west Limerick were fertile regions where the ballad thrived. Roundabout the Cashen mouth where the river Feale flows to the sea, a wonderful ballad called 'The Sandhills of Kilmore' (much beloved of the late Diarmuid Ó Catháin of Lixnaw) was hugely popular. I recall a few lines:

> We had one O'Neill from Boherbawn who is now in
>   Australia's shore
> He helped us swell our Fenian ranks on the Sandhills of Kilmore.

In the latter part of the nineteenth century songs of whiteboys and the Land League came to the fore. I particularly like the ballad called 'The Boys that left Rathea', an example of the power of the ballad giving a timely warning to all land grabbers!

> Healy and McDonnell 'tis well they had it planned
> To send McElligott to America and then to grab his land.
> But if McDonnell grabs the land he will surely meet the men
> That will take away his blessed life beside some lonely glen.

'The Vales of New Dirreen' is also a particularly fine emigration song and Donie Lyons of Glin, Co. Limerick, gives it a wonderful interpretation:

> Like John Mitchel in his cell, something tells to me
> That the dear old home is mine no more
>   round the vales of New Dirreen.

I could never understand how the word 'new' got into the song but I was told that in fact the original song was the Vales of 'you' Dirreen but it became corrupted to New Dirreen. This seems a logical explanation as there is certainly no place in the Athea region of Co. Limerick which is called New Direen.

The War of Independence and the Civil War were fertile grounds for the ballad maker and ballad singer. I recall a travelling singer by the name of John Wilson singing 'The Valley of Knockanure' on the street during the Listowel races in the 1940s and accompanying himself on the melodeon. I watched as tears flowed down the faces of some of his spellbound listeners. The famous Dublin balladeer, Frank Harte, acknowledged that it was hearing this song that started him on the ballad road.

During the 1930s and 1940s the ballad went out of style and was reviled by all save the 'hanam an diabhails' who kept the tradition alive in Corkery's hidden Ireland. My late father devised a platform for the launching of ballads on Radio Éireann with a programme called The Ballad Maker's Saturday Night. In my view the popularity of this programme gave a huge fillip to the reawakening and revival of interest in the ballad in the 1950s.

I suppose I was a rock and roll kid in those days, but in a few short years I recognised the innate worth of the ballad and began to collect and sing traditional songs myself. It was many years later that I followed in my father's footsteps and began to compose ballads. My father must have composed anything up to fifty ballads in his time. He bequeathed the copyright of these to me, so I feel it incumbent upon myself some day to undertake the task of publishing them all. Perhaps his most popular composition was the aforementioned 'Valley of Knockanure', printed, along with numerous other of his compositions, by Robert Cuthbertson, the Listowel printer. The multicoloured ballad sheets were sold at fairs, races and matches by the travelling people up and down the length and breadth of our land.

My father also recorded hundreds of songs on a wire recorder – the forerunner of the tape recorder – and while it was useful, the continuous snapping of the wire, which needs re-splicing, was an annoying feature.

As a result of the success of *The Ballad Maker's Saturday Night* our house was inundated with ballads from all corners of the country. With the arrival of The Clancys and the multiplicity of other ballad singers in the 1960s, the ballad, I believe, was saved forever.

Wrestlers, athletes, greyhounds, footballers, matches, ambushes, cuckoo clocks, the Shannon scheme, Superman, fountains, sheep, pigs, horses, ladies, rivers, mountains, hills and All-Irelands, were but a few of the many topics of which ballads were made. I have even collected a song called 'The Workhouse of Ra'kale' which bemoans the fact that the workhouse in Rathkeale was closed and presumably moved, lock stock and barrel, to Newcastlewest to be re-christened St Ita's Hospital in later times. The chorus goes:

Hurrah for the tramps of Ireland
Hurrah, hurroo, hurree
And down with those spalpeen hirelings
Who boss the LGB. [Local Government Board]

In the Newcastlewest area we had two famous ballad makers called T. D. Shanahan and Michael Scanlon. The latter was known as the poet laureate of Fenianism and wrote 'The Jackets Green' and 'Out and make way for the bold Fenian men'.

Jer Histon of Athea was another well known balladeer who wrote a wonderful rabelaisian song called 'The Lovely Banks of Blaine'. I also collected a very interesting song from the late Dr Edwards of Kilmallock called 'The Die Hard', the first verse of which went:

I am not a lot to look at just a diehard on the run
One of those inside a trench coat with bandolier and gun
You will know me when you see me watching round a dug out door
For I am a Kerry number one and Irish to the core.

To quote my late father again on ballads: 'The ballad may be compared to a man with a tar brush painting with bold strokes on a white-washed wall. It is simplicity itself in the story it tells and yet it often leads its hearer into a complex maze of human emotions. It can smash its way to the centre of the most select vestry or aesthetic circles and with a few words can peel off layer after layer of pseudo-cultural laminations.'

Another fertile ground for the balladeer was the so-called 'servant boy' having a go at his farmer employer:

It's well I remember I bet a half gallon
The hardship I suffered from June until May
With a roaring old farmer called Snuff and Cut Muggin
Who lived a few miles at the East of Athea.

The author of this is unknown as is the author of another song I collected from Jack Saunders of Newcastlewest called 'The Hiring Fair'. Its simplicity is touching indeed:

The hiring it commences about half past one I think
And when the farmer hires his girl, he'll take her for a drink
He'll then pick up her bundle and take her in for tea
And tell her we'll be leaving about half past three.
And when she reach her residence she will then take off her shawl
The missus she will order her to feed the calves and all
First to drink your tea and then we'll milk the cow
And for fear you might forget it throw a few mangolds to the sow.

Now there is social history encapsulated in a couple of quatrains of rural verse!

When I was growing up, if a ballad singer started to sing in a pub he would instantly be shouted down and the cry would be, 'why doesn't that fellow shut up'. I have lived to see the day when silence will be called for, and readily given, the minute a song is forthcoming in any social gathering – progress indeed!

Seán McCarthy of Finuge was another wonderful balladeer and I recall some of his moving and touching ballads with great affection. I must also mention Dan Keane of Moyvane some of whose ballads have won first place at Fleadh Cheoil na hÉireann. I have been listening, singing and collecting ballads for over fifty years and when I think I know all the songs of west Limerick and north Kerry I am rocked back on my heels to discover a song which I had not heard before. I would entreat any of my readers to ensure that any song that they may have is put in print so that it will not be lost for future generations. Many, thankfully, have appeared in print in local journals, where they are safe for posterity because 'bad ink is better than a good memory'.

In writing and singing ballads I feel I am continuing in that wonderful tradition which Isaac Walton spoke about so lovingly in 1653 and, no matter how technology advances, I have little doubt but that in another 350 years the unaccompanied ballad singer and the ballad maker and his song will still hold his indigenous and unique position in the heart of rural Ireland. It is exhilarating and uplifting to the spirit to be part of such a tradition in this third millennium. I have mentioned but a few of the songs of north Kerry and west Limerick in this little article but there are hundreds of them which, like the iceberg, lie seven-eighths under water. I finish with the truly memorable last verse of 'The Vales of New Direen':

And now to conclude these ill penned lines for fear I might be late
The morning train leaves Ardagh at twenty-five past eight
So God be with you old Ireland my starlit ocean queen
And a fond farewell to all who dwell in The Vales of New Direen.

In west Kerry when a singer finished a song he spoke these words 'Agus chuadar ag ól'. So what are you waiting for – off with you now!

CHAPTER SIX

Where History Meets Poetry: Bryan MacMahon and 'The Valley of Knockanure'

Gabriel Fitzmaurice

> If a man were permitted to make all the ballads, he need not care who should make the laws of a nation.
> – Andrew Fletcher of Saltoun (1653–1716), Scottish patriot.

According to this viewpoint, we are as influenced by the poetry of our nation as we are by its history, and more so than by its laws. In this light let us consider the ballads of the events of Thursday, 12 May 1921 at Gortaglanna in Knockanure, Co. Kerry.

The months of April and May 1921 saw a lot of bloodshed in the parish of what is now Moyvane-Knockanure near Listowel in north Kerry. This was, of course, during the Irish War of Independence. On Thursday 7 April Mick Galvin, an IRA volunteer, was killed by British forces during an ambush at Kilmorna in Knockanure. The IRA had been lying in wait to ambush a group of British soldiers who were cycling to Listowel after a visit to Sir Arthur Vicars at Kilmorna House, his residence. Vicars had been Ulster king of arms and custodian of the Irish crown jewels at the time of their burglary from Dublin Castle in 1907. Although he was never seriously suspected of being involved in their theft, it led to his ruin and, ultimately, to his death.

Found guilty of negligence and dismissed from his post, ruined socially and financially, with neither position nor pension, Vicars, at the invitation of his half-brother, George Mahony, came to live in Kilmorna House. When George died in 1912, he left the estate to Sir Arthur's sister, Edith, who lived in London. She decided that Sir Arthur could live out his life in Kilmorna. That he remained there during the War of Independence when British forces and Sinn Féin activists were matching atrocities was foolhardy rather than courageous, and typical of the man who was generally regarded by the local people as a decent, if eccentric, gentleman. But he was also passing information on IRA activity to the British army.

On Thursday, 14 April 1921, Kilmorna House was raided by the local IRA. One of the party, Lar Broder, told the steward, Michael Murphy, that they had come to burn the house, which they proceeded to do. However, three members of the flying column led Vicars to the end of the garden and shot him. (One of his executioners, Jack Sheehan, was himself shot dead by the British army near Knockanure on May 26.)

On 12 May crown forces shot dead three members of the flying column at Gortaglanna, Knockanure, a short distance from Kilmorna. This is the incident that is commemorated in the various ballads that follow.

Poetry, particularly narrative poetry to which the ballad belongs, distorts historical fact for aesthetic reasons – these may be for the imperatives of narrative, for considerations of rhyme or metre, or for reasons of the poet's perceptions or sympathies. The ballads of the atrocity in Knockanure on 12 May 1921 are no different. No version gets the facts entirely right. All versions tell a basic story but even the most histori-cally accurate ballads distort the facts. Some, either from carelessness or ignorance, or from unrestrained fancy, depart from historical fact entirely.

The most famous ballad of the events is Bryan MacMahon's 'The Valley of Knockanure', written in 1946 – though, in the true spirit of tradition, its authorship is disputed. Let's clear this up immediately. On 16 August 1969, Pádraig Ó Ceallacháin, republican and retired principal teacher of Knockanure national school, wrote the following testimony:

> I, Pádraig Ó Ceallacháin, formerly Príomh-Oide Scoile of Knockanure NS Co. Kerry hereby affirm that about 20 years ago I brought to Mr Bryan McMahon (*sic*) NT Ashe St Listowel a few verses of a traditional ballad on the murdering at Gortagleanna (*sic*) Co. Kerry in May 1921 of three soldiers of the Irish Republican Army – Jermiah (*sic*) Lyons, Patrick Dalton and Patrick Walsh. I also supplied Bryan McMahon with a copy of the sworn statement of Con Dee the survivor and requested him to rewrite the ballad and to add whatever verses were necessary so that it would be historically accurate. This Bryan McMahon did and later supplied me with printed copies of the ballad in question 'The Valley of Knockanure' a copy of which is affixed herewith.
> Signed: Pádraig Ó Ceallacháin
> Date: 16/8/69
> Witness: Aibhistín Ua Ceallacháin

The Valley of Knockanure (Co. Kerry)

In memory of Jeremiah Lyons, Patrick Dalton and Patrick Walsh, murdered by Crown Forces at Gortagleanna, Co. Kerry on 12 May 1921

You may sing and speak about Easter Week or
the heroes of Ninety-Eight,
Of the Fenian men who roamed the glen in victory or defeat,
Their names are placed on history's page, their memory will endure,

Not a song is sung for our darling sons in the Valley of Knockanure.

Our hero boys they were bold and true, no counsel would they take,
They rambled to a lonely spot where the Black and Tans did wait,
The Republic bold they did uphold though outlawed on the moor,
And side by side they bravely died in the Valley of Knockanure.

There was Walsh and Lyons and Dalton, boys, they were young and
in their pride,
In every house in every town they were always side by side,
The Republic bold they did uphold though outlawed on the moor,
And side by side they bravely died in the Valley of Knockanure.

In Gortagleanna's lovely glen, three gallant men took shade,
While in young wheat, full, soft and sweet the summer breezes played,
But 'twas not long till Lyons came on, saying
'Time's not mine nor your',
But alas 'twas late and they met their fate
in the Valley of Knockanure.

They took them then beside a fence to where the furze did bloom,
Like brothers so they faced the foe for to meet their dreadful doom,
When Dalton spoke his voice it broke with a passion proud and pure,
'For our land we die as we face the sky in the Valley of Knockanure.'

'Twas on a neighbouring hillside we listened in calm dismay,
In every house in every town a maiden knelt to pray,
They're closing in around them now with rifle fire so sure,
And Dalton's dead and Lyons is down in the Valley of Knockanure.

But ere the guns could seal his fate Con Dee had broken through,
With a prayer to God he spurned the sod and against the hill he flew,
The bullets tore his flesh in two, yet he cried with passion pure,
'For my comrades' death, revenge I'll get,
in the Valley of Knockanure.'

There they lay on the hillside clay for the love of Ireland's cause,
Where the cowardly clan of the Black and Tan had showed them
England's laws,
No more they'll feel the soft winds steal o'er uplands fair and sure,
For side by side our heroes died in the Valley of Knockanure.

I met with Dalton's mother and she to me did say,
'May God have mercy on his soul who fell in the glen today,
Could I but kiss his cold, cold lips, my aching heart 'twould cure,
And I'd gladly lay him down to rest in the Valley of Knockanure.'

The golden sun is setting now behind the Feale and Lee,
The pale, pale moon is rising far out beyond Tralee,
The dismal stars and clouds afar are darkened o'er the moor,
And the banshee cried where our heroes died
in the Valley of Knockanure.

Oh, Walsh and Lyons and Dalton brave, although your hearts are clay,
Yet in your stead we have true men yet to guard the gap today,
While grass is found on Ireland's ground your memory will endure,
So God guard and keep the place you sleep and
the Valley of Knockanure.

It's clear from this that the words we now sing, whatever about their ancestry, are Bryan MacMahon's.

Let us compare this, the best version, and closest to historical fact, with the actual history of the event as given first hand by Con Dee, the survivor of the atrocity:

Sworn Statements on the Incidents at Gortaglanna made by Con Dee Before Thomas R. Hill, J.P., Tarbert, in June 1921.

About nine-thirty a.m. on Thursday, May twelfth, 1921, I Cornelius Dee, accompanied by Patrick Dalton and Patrick Walsh [Dee's first cousin], left Athea unarmed, where we had been attending a mission given by the Redemptorist Fathers. We were walking along the road leading to Listowel when at Gortaglanna bridge we met Jerry Lyons; he was cycling. He dismounted and began talking about various happenings. After a few minutes Paddy Walsh suggested that we should go into a field as it would be safer than the road-side. We moved and were just inside the fence when we heard the noise of a lorry. 'Take cover, lads,' I advised, and we tried to conceal ourselves as best we could. Jerry Lyons, Paddy Dalton and I took cover immediately. Paddy Walsh ran to the end of a field and lay down. Very soon we were surrounded by men in the uniforms of the Royal Irish Constabulary. 'We are done, Connie,' said Paddy Dalton. 'Come out, lads,' I said, 'with our hands up.' Jerry Lyons, Paddy Dalton and myself stood with our hands over our heads. Paddy Walsh ran towards us. We were met with a torrent of abuse and foul language. I remember such expressions as 'Ye murderers', 'Ye b-------', 'We have got the real root', 'We have got the flying column'. We were asked our names and gave them correctly; we were searched and found unarmed, having nothing but a copy of the *Irish Independent*.

We were then compelled to undress and while we were fastening our clothes again we were beaten with rifles, struck with revolvers and thrown on the ground and kicked in trying to save ourselves. Then we were separated some distance from each other; four or five men came round each of us and my captors continued to beat me with their rifles and hit me with their fists. After about twenty minutes we were marched towards the road and then to the lorries. Paddy Walsh and Paddy Dalton were put in the first lorry. I was put in the second, and Jerry Lyons in the third. The lorries were then driven for about a half a mile towards Athea. They were then stopped and turned round. Paddy Walsh and Paddy Dalton were changed to the lorry in which I was. Jerry Lyons was not changed out of the last lorry, which was now leading. The lorries were then driven back the same road for about a mile. We were then ordered out of them. I looked at my companions; I saw blood on Jerry Lyons' face and on Paddy Walsh's mouth. Paddy Dalton was bleeding from the nose. We were then asked to run but we refused. We were again beaten with the rifles and ordered into a field by the roadside. We refused but were forced into the field. We asked for a trial but the Black and Tans laughed and jeered and called us murderers.

We were put standing in line facing a fence about forty yards from the road. I was placed first on the right, Jerry Lyons was next, Paddy Dalton next, and Paddy Walsh on the left. Then a Black and Tan with a rifle resting on the fence was put in front of each of us, about five yards distant. There were about ten more Black and Tans standing behind them. I looked straight into the face of the man in front of me. He delayed about twenty seconds as if he would like one of his companions to fire first. The second Black and Tan fired. Jerry Lyons flung up his arms, moaned and fell backwards. I glanced at him and noticed blood coming on his waistcoat; I turned round and ran. I was gone about twelve yards when I got wounded in the right thigh. My leg bent under me, but I held on running although I had to limp. I felt that I was being chased and I heard the bullets whizzing past me.

One of the lorries was driven along the road on my front and fire was maintained from it. After I had run for about a mile and a half I threw away my coat, collar, tie and puttees. The Tans continued to follow me for fully three miles. When too exhausted to run further, I flung myself into a drain in an oats garden. I was there about forty-five minutes when two men came along. They assisted me to walk for about forty yards. I was limping so much that one of them sent for a car and I was taken to a house.

I recognised Head Constable Smith, Listowel, along with the Black and Tans present at the massacre; also Constable Raymond, and there was one in the uniform of a district inspector of the Royal Irish Constabulary.

The official report issued on 14 May 1921 from the Dublin Castle publicity department reads as follows:

Three R.I.C. tenders were ambushed by about 100 armed men at
Kilmorna near Listowel at 1.15 p.m. on Thursday (May 12th).
Two R.I.C. were slightly wounded. The dead bodies of three
unknown rebels were found at the scene of the ambush, and it is
believed they suffered heavy casualties. Crown forces also captured a number of shot-guns, revolvers and ammunition.

Years later, in 1958, Con Dee was to revisit the tragedy in an
article he wrote in The Shannonside Annual. In it, he tells us
that, due to an outbreak of scabies, or 'IRA itch' as it was called
at the time, among members of the north Kerry flying column
in early May 1921, it was decided to disperse the flying column
in groups of three or four to get medical treatment. Paddy
Walsh, Paddy Dalton and Con Dee consisted of one group.
Paddy Walsh insisted that the three go to his home in Gunsboro in the parish of Ballydonoghue, 'the hub of activity for
North Kerry' according to Con Dee. This they did.

Shortly afterwards, Dee writes in that article:

a volunteer by the name of Buckley from Listowel came to Walsh
with a dispatch, which stated that a conversation of a certain
woman in Listowel with the police was overheard by a barmaid.
The woman told the police that a Mission was being held in
Athea, and that it was more than likely that the West Limerick
Column would be attending devotions there. She also said that
she would get all the information she could from a friend of hers
who had a religious goods stand at the Mission. When I relayed
the message to the others, we decided under no circumstances
would we let the West Limerick Column be trapped. We agreed
that Paddy Dalton [a native of Athea] and I should proceed at
once to Athea …

Dalton and I decided we'd make faster time if we travelled
without arms. We felt time was of the utmost importance to fore-

warn our comrades. We travelled by way of Tullamore, Knockanure, along the river Gale to Kilbaha, where we stopped at Han-
rahan's and had some refreshments. We continued along the river
as far as possible, and then cut across and arrived in Athea about
three o'clock in the afternoon.

We visited our good friend, Josie Liston, and told her our
mission. She immediately got in touch with the West Limerick
Column and local volunteers. That evening we contacted the
local mailman and made arrangements to meet him next morning
to censor the mail.

[Dee and Dalton went to the devotions in Athea] 'for at no
time at all,' [Dee continues,] 'did any of the fighting men miss an
opportunity to attend church if at all possible. After devotions
Patrick Dalton and I visited the Fathers who were staying at
Danaher's Hotel. We told them also of our mission. They became
angry to think such a thing could happen, and wanted to have the
woman put out of the village right away, but we objected as we
figured we might get some information from the mails. We
attended devotions for three nights and visited the priests until
eleven o'clock each night ...

Paddy Dalton's home was about a mile from the village and
each night we went there. I well remember the first night we were
going home, when we were a short distance from the house, Paddy
remarked that the family was still up. I asked him how he knew,
he remarked that they were looking at the cattle. Again I asked,
'How do you know?' He replied, 'Don't you see the lights in and
out of the cow house?' I did not see the light. When we got to the
house we went to his father's room and asked him if he had been
out. His father replied, 'No'. He then went to the other rooms and
asked his brothers. He received the same answer, 'No'. The next
morning we got up early and while at breakfast started to discuss
the lights of the night before. No one paid much attention to it,
but Paddy himself.

The routine the next night was the same. We went to devotions, visited the priests and started for home about the same

time. The same thing happened. Paddy again saw the lights, but I did not. He again questioned his people, but they again replied that they had not been out with a light. He wasn't satisfied till we went out and looked all over. We could see or hear nothing and went to bed.

The next day we were joined by Patrick Walshe (sic) in the village. We again attended the mission, went to confession, visited the priests and left for Paddy's home.

Again when approaching the house, Patrick Dalton and Patrick Walshe both saw the lights. I didn't see them. When the family was again questioned, they replied the same as the two previous nights. This time the two Patricks went out and searched but found nothing. The next morning the lights were again discussed. It was passed off as a joke. This was Thursday, 12 May.

Now let us consider some other ballads of the atrocity. *The Clancy Brothers and Tommy Makem Song Book* (Tiparm Music Publishers, Inc., New York, 1964) prints a much truncated, though essentially Bryan MacMahon's, version of 'The Valley of Knockanure'. Historical inaccuracies creep in: 'But e'er (sic) the guns could seal his fate, young Walsh had broken thro'' (it was Dee who escaped), and 'The summer sun is sinking low behind the field and lea' (it should be 'Feale and Lee', two local rivers). This displays an ignorance of local history and geography, understandable in the mutating nature of a folk ballad, but historically inexcusable.

The spalpeen poet, Paddy Drury (1865–1945), a native of Knockanure, wrote a number of ballads about the atrocity. One of his versions, 'The Dawning of the Day', is less a narrative of the events than a vehicle for his own anti-English, pro-de Valera, anti-Treaty sentiments. Though it is not possible to date its composition, it clearly originates from a time when 'Kerrymen are fighting still' before de Valera, as leader of the IRA, can say 'lay down your guns, the fight is won', and before the same de Valera, as taoiseach of the Irish Free State government in the early 1940s, executed Kerrymen Maurice O'Neill of Caherciveen and Charlie Kerins of Tralee for IRA activity.

The Dawning of the Day

O, Holy Ireland, suffering still,
Your troubles now are great,
From tyrants trained to shoot and kill
Whose minds are filled with hate;
Who sold their souls for foreign gold
To rob and steal away;
It's no wonder that our hearts are sad
At the dawning of the day.

Sons of North Kerry, proud and true,
Step forward every man;
You know the foreign bloodhound crew,
The murderous Black and Tan
Who shot young Lyons and Dalton
And Walsh the proud and gay
As they left their gallant comrades
At the dawning of the day.

On Gortaglanna's rugged height
Surrounded by that crew
How could they stand, how could they fight,
What could our martyrs do?
They showed no fear when death was near,
When the tigers sought their prey,
But our blood ran cold when the tale was told
At the dawning of the day.

But Kerrymen are fighting still
From Dingle to Tralee;
I'm proud to be a Kerryman
And I'm proud of sweet Athea;
I'm proud of Lyons, that noble lad
Who gave his life away
As he left his gallant comrades
At the dawning of the day.

When writing down the Roll of Fame
In old Ireland's history,
With green and gold illume the name
Of gallant brave Con Dee;
I'd give my life to clasp his hand
And 'tis with him I would stay
And fight by his side for my native land
At the dawning of the day.

The above is the version given by Jeremiah Histon in his article 'I Remember Paddy Drury' printed in *The Shannonside Annual* of 1957. Jack Carroll of Listowel, a respected traditional singer and a reliable source of local ballads, had the following concluding verse which I collected from him in the 1970s:

Oh Mother Ireland, dry your tears
Be ever full of cheer,
Pray for those noble volunteers
Who fought to set you free.
When freedom comes to Ireland's sons
De Valera* he will say,
'Lay down your guns, the fight is won'
At the dawning of the day.

*In politically sensitive company, Jack would change the de Valera reference to:

> When freedom comes to Ireland's sons
> Brave Irishmen will say
> 'Lay down your guns, the fight is won'
> At the dawning of the day.

Another of Drury's versions goes as follows:

The Glen of Knockanure

> May the Lord have mercy on their souls,
> Their hearts were loyal and true,
> They were beat and shot in a lonely spot
> In a glen near Knockanure.

> There was Jerry Lyons, now, from Duagh,
> There was Dalton from Athea,
> There was Walsh from Ballydonoghue
> And Con Dee who ran away.

> Through hill and vale he did leg bail
> As the bullets pierced the ground
> Till he jumped the stream at the Bog Lane
> Where he blinked the devil's hounds.

> Through mountainside he did tide
> Though wounded then and sore
> And he shed a tear for his comrades dear
> Who were bleeding in their gore.

> For our martyrs bold, now dead and cold,
> To the lorries were thrown in

And Smith said there was an ambush at
The Gortaglanna glen.

For now Sinn Féin prove that you'll gain
And remember those who died
And let each man try to keep his eye
On Smith* and on McBride*.

Now we have two more we sad deplore
That in this parish fell,
They are Galvin and Sheehan.
In Heaven they all dwell.

(*Smith and McBride were two of the Black and Tans/RIC
who were present at Gortaglanna on that day).

Tim Leahy of Mount Rivers, Listowel also composed a
ballad. His version, written on 20 September 1921, is printed
in Colm Ó Lochlainn's More Irish Street Ballads, first published
in 1965 by The Three Candles, Dublin, and subsequently, in
1978, by Pan Books, London. This is a faithful version of the
events at Gortaglanna. What it lacks in drama and personality,
it makes up for in local detail, details that other versions don't
give us – for instance, he tells us that the boys were coming
from mass that morning and that they were waiting for a dispatch. There is no evidence of this in Con Dee's testimony nor
is it mentioned by Danny MacMahon, who was working close
to home in Gortaglanna on that day, in his account of their
capture published in J. Anthony Gaughan's Listowel and its
Vicinity (Mercier Press, Cork, 1973). Leahy alone also tells us
that they were shot near an ancient ringfort which, inciden-
tally, is still to be seen in front of the ditch where they were
shot and where now stands the monument erected to their

memory by the North Kerry Republican Soldiers Memorial Committee in 1949. Here is his ballad:

The Valley of Knockanure

It was in the year of 'twenty-one,
All in the month of May,
Some of our noble Column boys
Were strolling on their way.
They came from Mass that morning,
Their souls were now secure,
But little they thought that they'd be shot
In the Valley of Knockanure.

On a bridge near Gortaglanna
Those boys a rest did take;
They were waiting a dispatch to say
What move they were to make;
With feelings strong to move along
And make themselves secure –
But it was their lot that day to be caught
In the Valley of Knockanure.

Now when those boys were taken,
They were beaten black and blue;
Into the lorries they were thrown –
Alas! What could they do?
They dare not ask for mercy now
But they prayed they might endure
Their torments for their Motherland
In the Valley of Knockanure.

Those heroes' names I'll now relate
Who were captured on that day:

Paddy Walsh and Jerry Lyons
And Dalton from Athea;
Con Dee from Ballylongford
He surprised the Tans I'm sure
When he made that dash for liberty
From the Valley of Knockanure.

Near an ancient fort those boys were shot
And there their bodies lay
Till Ireland's sons a tomb will raise
To them some future day.
So pray the Lord may grant them rest,
Their souls with him secure,
For a martyr's death those heroes met
In the Valley of Knockanure.

What woe and grief to parents came
That night when told the tale
In every house they knelt and prayed
Along the River Gale
For those gallant boys who gave their lives
Our freedom to secure
And relieve Con Dee that wounded be
In the Valley of Knockanure.

And now to the version where history and poetry part company entirely, the version recorded from Joe Heaney (Seosamh Ó hÉanaí) by Ewan MacColl and Peggy Seeger in their home in Beckenham, Kent, England in 1964. Joe, by way of giving background information, has the following to say:

You know in Ireland every six months, the priest comes around to give advice and confessions to the old people, you see, in the cottages. And there's one particular house they come to every time. Well this day they came to Knockanure in County Kerry and it was in 1922 and there was two wee lads, Éamonn Dalton and Danny Walsh was on the run up in the hills and five lorry loads of Black and Tans came to hunt them. And they had a boy, a fourteen year old boy called Con Dee bringing them messages to tell them how the Tans was behaving and the Tans, fifty Tans, [a] hundred Tans, I should say, surrounded them with rifles and they told Con Dee to get away somewhere and bring a message to the village that they were willing to die to save the village. And the two fellows died. But the people, the old people coming, as they do there, they come along, old women and men and to spare them, the two lads fought to the death with a hundred Black and Tans up on the hill and saved the village from ruin, because if they ran back to the village, the lads were afraid the Tans would come back and probably kill innocent people.

And he sings:

> You may boast and speak about Easter Week
> Or the heroes of 'ninety-eight,
> Of the gallant men who roamed the glen
> To victory or defeat.
> The men who died on the scaffold high
> Were outlawed on the moor.
> Not a word was spoken of two young lads
> In the Valley of Knockanure.
>
> 'Twas on a summer's evening
> Those two young lads sat down.
> They were waiting on a brief dispatch
> To come from Tralee town.
> It wasn't long till Lyons came on
> Saying 'Time's not mine nor yours,
> Look out we are surrounded
> In the Valley of Knockanure.'

Young Dalton grabbed a rifle
And by Walsh's side he stood.
He gazed across the valley
And over toward the hill.
In the glen where armed men
With rifles fired galore,
There were Dalton, Dan and the Black and Tans
In the Valley of Knockanure.

One shot from Dalton's rifle
Sent a machine gun out of play.
He turned to young Lyons and said
'Now try and get away.
Keep wide of rocks, keep close to nooks
And cross by Freeney's moor,
And Danny and I will fight or die
In the Valley of Knockanure.'

The summer sun was sinking fast
On Kerry by the sea.
The pale moon it was rising
Over sweet Tralee.
The twinkling stars they shone so far
Out on the dreary moor,
And when Dalton died, the Banshee cried
In the Valley of Knockanure.

God bless our bold Sinn Féiners
Wherever they may be.
Don't forget to kneel and pray
For that hero brave Con Dee.
He ran among the Kerry hills
To the rich man and the poor,
Salt tears he shed for those he left dead
In the Valley of Knockanure.

Our hero boys were stout and bold,
No counsel would they take,
They ran among the lonely glens
Where the Black and Tans did lay,
The women of the uplands
Gazed out across the moor
Watching Dalton and Dan fighting fifty to one
In the Valley of Knockanure.

And 'twas God who sent those boys to life
But did not say how long,
For well we knew that England's crew
Would shoot them right or wrong.
With our rifles fixed right up to fire
And bullets quick and sure,
We'll have revenge for those young men
In the Valley of Knockanure.

Young Éamonn Dalton and Danny Walsh
Were known both far and wide,
On every hill and every glen
They were always side by side.
A republic bold they did uphold,
They were outlawed on the moor,
And side by side they fought and died
In the Valley of Knockanure.

I met with Dalton's mother,
Those words to me did say,
'May the Lord have mercy on my son,
He was shot in the getaway.
If I only could kiss his cold, cold lips
My aching heart would cure
And I'd lay his body down to rest
In the Valley of Knockanure.'

This has more to do with Hollywood than history and it calls into question the great singer's authority in matters historical. It calls into question, too, the historical authority of folk song. Basically, as we all know, song is not history. Nonetheless, Joe Heaney's version demonstrates how history becomes legend. And we need legend. Though historically inaccurate, legends express the spirit of their people, that indefinable coming together of historical fact, memory, story, song and poetry that make us what we are.

Nowadays, the events of April and May 1921 are almost entirely forgotten, even in the parish of Moyvane-Knockanure where they occurred. Galvin, Vicars, Dalton, Lyons, Walsh, Dee and Sheehan are scarcely remembered. Some may welcome this amnesia as a good thing. But amnesia is never good. We forget our history at our peril. We censor our poetry to our cost. Let a poet have the final word. Art Ó Maolfabhail, writing in his poem 'Inis Córthaidh agus Gné den Stair', about Enniscorthy and the events of 1798, states that '*ní mór peacaí ró-ghránna/na staire a mhaitheamh*' ('the ugly sins/of history must be pardoned').

We must forgive history's ugly sins. But to forgive them, we must first know what they are.

CHAPTER SEVEN

Bryan MacMahon, Peig Sayers and the Publication of Peig in English

Mícheál de Mórdha

Tabharfaidh mé cúntas anseo ar conas mar a foilsíodh an t-aistriúchán Béarla den leabhar *Peig* agus an cúlra a bhí ag baint leis sin.[1] Ar ndóigh is é Bryan MacMahon an t-údar iomráit-each ó Lios Tuathail a rinne an t-aistriúchán. Foilsíodh an leagan Béarla de *Pheig* sa bhliain 1973, céad bliain go díreach ó saolaíodh *Peig*, agus is iad an Talbot Press a d'fhoilsigh. Is féidir a rá gur comhoibriú agus toradh fiúntach ba ea an t-aistriúchán sin idir dhá thraidisiúin mhóra liteartha Chorca Dhuibhne agus Chiarraí Thuaidh.

To begin this chapter I would like to refer to certain strong sociocultural and linguistic connections between the Dingle peninsula and north Kerry of which the publication of the English language version of *Peig* is a prime example. The 'cross-pollination of culture' between the two areas has been going on for ever and ever. When the Irish language was the *lingua franca* all around the county the two areas were linguistically bonded. Up to this very day it is quite apparent that the Irish language is the source of many expressions and idioms found in ordinary speech in the north of this county. Indeed this is so in most rural communities in this country.

Naomh Bréanainn (St Brendan), the seafaring saint revered in both west and north Kerry, and indeed all around this 'Kingdom', is another strong connection. His mother, Cara, was of the *corca Dhuibhne*, the inhabitants of the Dingle peninsula, and Bréanainn, who was born in the vicinity of Fenit, is reputed to have been a regular visitor to his mother's people on the peninsula. It is more than likely that his visits to his maternal relatives were made by sea, thus sowing the seed for his epic journeys later in his life. When he embarked on his American voyage he chose Cuas a' Bhodaigh (Brandon Creek), at the foot of Mount Brandon, as his point of embarkation.[2]

In the nineteenth century and beyond several young men of very little means from west Kerry worked as 'spailpíní' in the more affluent north Kerry, where the farmers could afford some extra labour. As we know, the poor 'spailpíní' worked for a pittance. One of their number was Seán Ó Duinnshléibhe, the nineteenth-century Blasket poet of some fame. In one of his compositions, 'Bó na bPóilíní', he refers to 'Ó dTórna' (the vicinity of Abbeydorney):

Nuair a chuadar isteach chun an landlady a dhíol,
D'ardaigh na fairies an bhó leo,
D'ardaíodar leo í mar a bheadh ceo ag imeacht le gaoith,
Mórthimpeall Chruach Mhárthan is Mám Clasach síos,
Tá sí i bpáirc leasa ag tál bhainne ar mhná sí,
I mbaile in íochtar Ó dTórna.[3]

There was a very strong tradition in west Kerry of persons making the pilgrimage on foot to 'Tobar na Molt' in north Kerry and making the return journey in one day. Peig Sayers herself describes a trip to Tobar na Molt (Wether's Well) in her book.[4]

One of the most enduring tales available in printed form is that of a north Kerry woman, surnamed Pierce, walking her cow all the way from Ballyheigue to the townland of Ceathrú, in Dún Chaoin, in order to settle down and get married there. The cow was apparently her dowry. In his book, *Ag Tagairt don Scéal* (FNT 1973), Tomás Luibhéad, an author and playwright from Leath Taoibh, near Ballyferriter, tells us that this woman is actually his great-grandmother.[5] Tomás' grandmother, another Peig Sayers, was born in Ceathrú, Dún Chaoin:[6]

> Ar an gCeathrúin, i bParóiste Dhún Chaoin, is ea a rugadh Neain. Sayers an sloinne a bhí uirthi, agus Peig a hainm baiste ... Pierce an sloinne a bhí ar mháthair Neain. Ba as Bhaile Uí Thaidhg, taobh amuigh de Thrá Lí, di.

On page fifty-five of the book the author gives his grandmother's account of how, on a May morning, her mother drove a cow all the way from Ballyheigue to Dún Chaoin, a journey by road of over forty miles, in one day. She milked the cow three times along the way and she also had to deal with a rather amorous youth she met in Tralee. When he tried to have his evil way with her she gave him a kick on a certain part of his anatomy which left him prancing madly about the place for several hours and drove any bad ideas completely out of his head. This lively woman continued on her quest and arrived safely in Dún Chaoin as night was falling.

Before I spend all my time on this track I should really get into the subject matter of this chapter. Therefore I will endeavour to set the background to the publication of the English version of *Peig* in 1973.

The translator, Bryan MacMahon, of Listowel, is undoubtedly one of the most famous Kerrymen of the twentieth century. Peig Sayers, of the Great Blasket, is one of the most famous, or should we say, infamous, Kerry women of the same period. As a regular visitor to west Kerry, MacMahon was well aware of her fame as an author and storyteller. *Peig*, her autobiography, was published in her native Irish in 1936. As a fluent speaker of Irish himself, MacMahon would have had no difficulty whatsoever in following Peig's narrative.

In an address to the ninth annual seminar of the Canadian Association for Irish Studies, at Memorial University, Newfoundland in February 1976, Bryan MacMahon stated that he did not, however, know Peig as well as others:[7]

I knew Peig Sayers. Not indeed a fraction as well as others, but I saw enough of her to catch the essence of a brave and sensitive woman, whose voice lingers in my memory, whose face is almost indelibly imaged on the air before me, and whose rareness of spirit, sprung from her conviction that she was one of the last of a noble line, has thrust itself through the borders of the nations … True, towards the end of her days she complained that she was unrecognised but this was something of an exaggeration on her part. 'There will never again in Ireland be an old woman as Irish as me', she told me once in a plaint that is echoed in her work. By this she meant that there would never again live in Ireland a woman who had so indefatigably and eagerly committed to rote a vast storehouse of oral lore and who had held the key to this treasury in her mind and heart and tongue … Peig in her old age in Vicarstown, and in Dingle Hospital, certainly had visitors. I did not intrude a great deal upon her: I simply watched and memorised.

There is a passage in his book *Here's Ireland* in which MacMahon describes a visit to Peig in Dingle Hospital during an outing from his primary school in Listowel.[8] The pupils had been primed to pay due respect to the old woman who had been battling cancer of the mouth and was then sightless:

> An old woman sat up in bed in Dingle Hospital. Her hair was carefully combed.
>
> As she sat in state, her sightless eyes alternating with her ears in sifting the occasions of the ward, a flock of schoolboys crowded to the stairhead and spilled quietly into the room.
>
> As four boys walked forward, nuns and nurses watched carefully.
>
> One of the four boys spoke in Irish. 'Peig Sayers,' he said, 'we offer you this small gift as a mark of our esteem ... chun méid ár measa a chur in iúl duit.'
>
> He thrust his gift into the blind woman's hands.
>
> The tears came down the old features. Peig Sayers of the Blasket islands, one of the great narrators of wondertales of Gaelic Ireland, and a superb natural actress was on her deathbed.
>
> In gratitude she stretched out her hands to read and caress the boy's face.

This visit must have taken place around 1958, the year Peig died.[9] I wonder if any of those boys remember that episode to the present day?

Bryan MacMahon's numerous visits to the Corca Dhuibhne Gaeltacht commenced in the mid 1920s when, as a young boy, he spent a holiday with his parents, Patrick and Johanna, in the little townland of Corra Ghráig, near Feothanach. The MacMahons stayed with the Ó Muircheartaigh family. The lady of the house, Mrs Annie Uí Mhuircheartaigh, was a very polished speaker of Irish. The Listowel man once reminisced on a Raidió na Gaeltachta programme that Bean Uí Mhuircheartaigh's clear diction and turn of phrase as she spoke Irish fluently and effortlessly often echoed in his ears in later life.[10] It did not take him long to get acquainted, even at a tender age, with local characters. In the same interview he explains how he received an impromptu lesson in Irish from Parthalán Ó Cinnéide, a renowned local teacher, during his first sojourn to the heart of the Gaeltacht. He subsequently met other local characters who willingly assisted him in his quest to become a fluent speaker of the native tongue. Not that the young Bryan was ignorant of Irish. His grandmother, Margaret (née Creed) MacMahon, was a fluent Irish speaker often visited by folklore collectors. His father was also fluent in the native *lingua*. A travelling language teacher, Tomás Ó Donnchú, visited the primary school in Listowel where Bryan was a very young pupil in 1919 and was permitted to give a lesson in Irish after school – young Bryan attended and took to the language immediately. Ó Donnchú 'was out in 1916' and was a 'fear uasal' according to his pupil. In later life Bryan MacMahon became acquainted with the Shelta or the Cant, the secret language of the travelling people, and undoubtedly his deep knowledge of Irish was of great assistance to him in acquiring fluency in it.

Having spent several holidays with the Ó Muircheartaigh family of Corra Ghráig the MacMahons found themselves a few miles away in the renowned Tigh Eibhlín on the shore of Smerwick Harbour – a guesthouse run with great diligence and discipline by the legendary Eibhlín Feiritéar.[11] Garry McMahon, Bryan's son, has written an excellent and evocative song in Irish about the same premises which he simply called 'Tigh Eibhlín'. It is often broadcast on Raidió na Gaeltachta.

Here in the heart of the west Kerry Gaeltacht Bryan MacMahon perfected his Irish and went forth to meet great west Kerry characters of the time including Maurice 'Kruger'

Kavanagh and Seán 'Charlie' Ó Conchúir, both of Dún Chaoin parish.[12]

He held Kruger in great regard and duly visited the ailing character in Dingle hospital in the early 1970s. As a result Kruger gave instructions to the staff of his pub in Dún Chaoin that Bryan MacMahon would be given free drink on his next visit to the hostelry. Of course, it was a well known fact that the Listowel man was a confirmed teetotaller but on the other hand Kruger's hospitality *was* often extended to friend and stranger alike. On another visit to his beloved west Kerry, Mac-Mahon, then the author of several books, was listening intently to a story being told to him by an old man near Dingle quay. A car drew up and a man stuck his head out the window and proffered a book to Bryan and brusquely asked him to sign the book, which turned out to be MacMahon's translation of *Peig*.

'What name will I put down?' asked Bryan in Irish.

'Criostóir Ó Rinn,' responded the other man.

The book was duly signed and the car moved away again. Bryan was so engrossed in the story that it did not immediately dawn on him that the man requesting his autograph was none other than Christy Ring himself. When he realised that he might have offended the late great Christy, in as much as he did not bid him the time of day, MacMahon went in hot pursuit and when eventually he caught up with him he began to explain to Ringy that he was so interested in the story that he was listening to that his attention could not be ·diverted elsewhere. Trying to explain the situation further the Kerryman asked the Corkman this rhetorical question: 'If you were taking a free and Cork a few points down, would you have taken any heed of me?'

'No, I would have taken the head off you!' declared Ringy.

(This is my translation of his narrative in Irish.)

That Bryan MacMahon is regarded as one of Kerry's and, indeed, Ireland's, greatest literary talents ever is in no dispute. On the other hand poor Peig has become a figure of hate for thousands of those who were forced to study her book for the leaving certificate. It was definitely a mistake, in my opinion, that *Peig* was placed on the leaving certificate curriculum and remained thereon for ages. It was unfair both to Peig and her students. Students in the latter half of the twentieth century, with all their mod cons, could not relate to the impoverished and deprived life, in their eyes, that the old woman from the Great Blasket went through. The fact that Peig was not actually the writer at all, but the author and brilliant storyteller, may not have been absorbed to any great effect by all the students who had to compulsorily and regimentally read her book.

Her book is still a choice for the leaving certificate and some schools continue to use it. But it is now very much a matter of choice and it is not imposed on every student. However, I feel that the true significance of Peig and her book can never be explained to leaving certificate students and it should be introduced at third level instead of second level education.

In latter years Peig's significance as a storyteller extraordinary has come to the fore and she is getting due recognition from scholars in this regard. One of the greatest folklore scholars of the last century, Bo Almqvist, emeritus professor of folklore at UCD, is working on the publication of several volumes of Peig's stories. This is a mammoth task as a vast number of stories have been collected from her. For example, Dr Seosamh Ó Dálaigh (better known as Joe Daly), himself from Peig's native parish of Dún Chaoin, collected some 300 stories from her repertoire on behalf of the Folklore Commission. These and hundreds more stories written down from Peig are stored intact in the vast repository of Cumann Bhéaloideas Éireann in UCD and elsewhere. If all her stories are eventually published this collection will undoubtedly be seen as one of the great folklore collections.

It has been recognised that Peig's stories, as they appear in her books, have been sanitised and subjectively edited by various individuals, including her son, Mícheál Ó Guithín, Maidhc Pheig Sayers or 'An File', to whom she dictated her life story. In the process of writing down and editing her stories the greatest part of Peig's virtuosity as an accomplished storyteller has been lost to a considerable extent. 'An File' has been accused of actually imposing his own ideas onto his mother's stories and anecdotes during the transcription process. I include here an extract from a lecture given by the broadcaster and film maker, Breandán Feiritéar, at the recent Ceiliúradh an Bhlascaoid:[13]

Deireadh tuataí tuisceannacha sa phobal ná raibh Maidhc ann in aon chor. Gurbh ionann Maidhc agus Peig, a mháthair. Deiridís gurb é Maidhc a scrígh féin-chuntas Pheig ar a saol féin – sa tslí sin go raibh breith a bhéil féin aige uirthi – gur bhreac sé an rud a thaitnigh leis agus an insint nár thaitnigh gur fhág sé ar lár é. Dá réir sin gur ionann Maidhc agus a mháthair. Dúirt Joe Daly go raibh cruthúnas eile fós aige féin gurbh ionann Maidhc agus Peig. Ach a raibh Peig in ospidéal an Daingin i mblianta deireanacha a saoil, ba mhinic a thug Joe marcaíocht ón Daingean do Mhaidhc is é ag dul ar tuairisc a mháthar. Lá des na laethanta seo gur chuadar ón Daingean le cois a chéile, chuadar ar dtúis go dtí an oispidéal ar thuairisc Pheig mar ar chaitheadar tamall cuideachtan ag caint is ag caibideal léi. Nuair a bhí an gnó san déanta chuadar faoi'n mbaile síos. Bhí allaíre nó bodhaire beag ar Mhaidhc – rud a rith le dúchas ins na Sayersaigh. Chuadar isteach go Tig Churráin, a dúirt Joe Daly, mar ar órdaíodar dhá scíobas dí dóibh féin. Tháinig sean-bhean an tí amach chun beannú dóibh agus chun fáiltithe rompu. Bheir sí ar láimh ar Mhaidic agus d'fhiafraigh go cneasta dó: 'Conas tá do mháthair, a Mhaidhc?' 'Sé an freagra a thug Maidhc uirthi – a dúirt Joe Daly – ná: 'Táim go maith, go raibh maith agat!'

To my knowledge there is no known visual recording of Peig in full spate reciting any of her stories. This is lamentable as a visual recording would have shown her as the accomplished storyteller she was and would have left no doubt as to her credentials in this field. There are audio recordings of her stories which give some indication of her prowess as a seanchaí or storyteller.[14]

She would have been amazed if not altogether astonished to have been in the last few years the subject of a TV documentary by Breandán Feiritéar[15] and also the subject of one of the Great Blasket Commemorations[16] and even the subject of a recent documentary on RTÉ Radio 1,[17] and several other programmes and articles since her death. Nowadays, she is being seen in a new light and in some respects as a pre-feminist by eminent scholars. There was a lot of notice taken of Professor Pat Coughlan from NUI Cork when she made pronouncements in this regard at the Blasket Commemoration of 1998. In the January 2003 documentary on RTÉ Radio 1 produced by Cathal Póirtéir there were some very pertinent declarations made about Peig Sayers and her significance as a storyteller. This documentary and further documentaries on the lives of Tomás Ó Criomhthain and Muiris Ó Súilleabháin and the abandonment of the Great Blasket are published on two CDs in the excellent production entitled *Blasket Reflections* (2003).[18]

Several scholars gave their opinions of Peig and her niche in twentieth-century Ireland. Declan Kiberd, professor of Anglo-Irish literature at NUI Dublin has this to say:

> Peig Sayers has suffered in one way by becoming a classroom illustration of a certain kind of Catholic, Gaelic Irishness. That was very unfair to her, she was her own woman and there are very interesting recent articles who read her as almost a pre-feminist, a woman who was tremendously beautiful but also as a woman who was also very self-sufficient, and had to be in order to survive in that world, she didn't get a house of her own until she was middle aged but brought up a whole lot of children in someone else's. And the key friendship in that book, the one with Cáit Jim, is of a kind now, which is frequently found in novels written by feminists and artists.
>
> I think she may be due for revival and a more broad-minded reading but of course what happened is that all of these Blasket books were co-opted by state forces, as surely as Muiris was by the Gardaí.
>
> They became in a sense the theoretical underpinning to de Valera's speech of maidens of the crossroads and so on. Now of course *An tOileánach* became too difficult for secondary students to study because the vocabulary is awesomely wide and accurate at the same time. Peig's was a bit more accessible and I think she suffered in a way in being exhibit A in that kind of version of Dev's Ireland because I can remember all the boys who sat by me in secondary school revolting against this as generations did. But what they were revolting against, if you think about it, isn't really the text, isn't really the woman or her personality, it's the use to which the particular text was put by that ideology at that time and of course that revolt began in 1941 with *An Béal Bocht*! And it's been going on ever since, it seems to me to have been very hard on the Blasket writers to stand sponsor over the baptismal font for Dev's Ireland.

In the same documentary Professor Pat Coughlan of NUI Cork gives us her interpretation of Peig as a woman:

> One thing we see in Peig is the relation within the community at large on the Blasket and from Dún Chaoin, but especially the woman-to-woman relation, and I think that is something that hasn't been written about or discussed, not just perhaps in *Peig* but in the discussion of Irish literature in general. I think that may be an area people may be more ready to understand and pay attention to; how the women depended on each other, and of course it's not always trouble free, for instance economic realities sometimes disrupt this. As in the well known section early in Peig's life, early in the narratives, Peig's sister-in-law, her eldest brother's wife, deeply resents Peig – this girl sitting around the house and saying she can go get her own house and find her own food and so on. Where Peig is forced to leave, as many young women were, and become a farm servant and a domestic servant, because the economy wasn't there to support her, this drives a wedge between the two women.
>
> But when she goes to the Blasket there's a conspicuous fellowship between her and the other new friends that she makes and between herself and her mother-in-law which I think we should acknowledge really and explore further. There's a lot more to be done about the accounts of women's lives in that community and also about the ideology that emerges in it because, as I've also argued, there's a lot of moments within the three narratives where jokingly and humorously the old idea that women are always talking and all they do is talk, where they're kind of nodded to and humorously included by Peig, but sometimes as it were in inverted commas, where she uses them as a put down, that the women have defeated the men and the only thing the men can find to say is 'you can't ever silence a woman'. So I think there is just more exploration that needs to be done, when I wrote the essay about these texts I just hoped, as I say at the end, that more people

perhaps better qualified than I am in the language would explore these issues and I think there are some issues certainly that women, historians, that feminists, that readers of women's literature will be interested in because *Peig* is among other things a very rare thing, we have very few women's autobiographies in Irish or English from Ireland and we should cherish the one we do have.

Perhaps the most knee-jerking revelation of all is uttered in this documentary by Padraig Ua Maoileoin, author grandson of Tomás Ó Criomhthain. Ua Maoileoin died in 2002, shortly before the programme was broadcast. He states:

> Bean ab ea Peig, bean a bhí baineann agus a bhí ceanúil ar fhearaibh, buíochas le Dia! Agus bhí an-mheas uirthi mar mhúin sí an-chuid ceachtanna do bhuachaillí an oileáin, agus gá acu leis ag an am mar ní raibh éinne acu ach a leithéid!

It would appear from this that Peig was into sex education long before the subject was formally introduced into our classrooms. The book *Peig* was published by the Talbot Press in 1936, when Peig was fifty-eight years of age. It is the best known of her three books and made her a household name. Her life and stories are also the subjects of *Machtnamh Seanmhná*[19] which was later translated as *An Old Woman's Reflections*.[20] Another book, *Beatha Pheig Sayers*, was published after Peig's death.[21] Kenneth Jackson published a volume of her stories entitled *Scéalta ón mBlascaod*.[22] Robin Flower also published stories from her repertoire.

Peig was fifteen years in her grave before the English translation of her book appeared. The fact that the book was not translated into English until almost forty years after its publication in Irish is something of a mystery when one considers that the other well known books from the Blasket, *An tOileánach* by Tomás Ó Criomhthain[23] and *Fiche Blian ag Fás* by Muiris Ó Súilleabháin[24] were relatively swiftly translated from the original Irish into English. In fact the English translation of *Fiche Blian ag Fás* was available before the Irish book was published but it was decided, and rightly so, that the Irish version would be published first.

Why then did it take so long to publish *Peig* in English? I have endeavoured to unravel some of this enigma without much success. It would appear that correspondence regarding the publication of the English version of *Peig* is difficult to access, if available at all. The Educational Company could not furnish any useful information as they have no documentation relating to the publication in their files.

All I have from my endeavours is an e-mail message from Clíona Ní Bhréartúin, senior editor with the Educational Company:

> An t-aon eolas ar féidir liom teacht air ná gur tugadh cead do Mercier Press eagrán Béarla a chur i gcló idir 1951 agus 1971 nuair a cuireadh an cead sin ar ceal arís … I mBealtaine 1974 tugadh cead do Syracuse University Press eagrán Meiriceánach a chur i gcló le clúdach cruaidh. I mí Meitheamh 1991 tugadh cead dóibh cóip le clúdach bog a chur i gcló. Is i Stáit Aontaithe Mheiriceá agus Ceanada a bhaineann an cead sin amháin.

From what I have learned it appears that a large amount of filed material from the Talbot Press was acquired by Professor Eoin Dudley Edwards of UCD when the press was acquired by the Smurfit Group. This material has since been deposited in the National Archives but has not yet been processed. However a cursory glance through the documents has not revealed anything of significance to our quest. Searching for further documentation could be a subject for a postgraduate student.

Kevin Etchingham, now an octogenarian and living in a Dublin suburb, who worked as a manager with the Talbot Press, is the person who eventually succeeded in having *Peig* translated into English. Mr Etchingham does not in any way seek credit for this but, only for his initiative, we may have had an even longer wait for *Peig* to appear in the second official language.

In June 2004, I interviewed him about his contribution to the publication. Asked his opinion as to why it took almost forty years for a translation of *Peig* to appear he intimated that it may have been thought desirable in certain quarters not to have an English translation even though everyone else desired it: 'Is dóigh liom go raibh gach éinne ag súil go mbeadh aistriúchán glan díreach ar Pheig chun nach mbeadh orthu a bheith bodhar – na scoláirí – leis an nGaeilge ... Tá a fhios agat ní leabhar ró-thaitneamhach é. Cuireadh amach é ag an Educational Company agus bhí sé fé mar a bhíodh na leabhair scoile fadó. Tá a fhios agat, ní raibh aon dearadh déanta orthu i gceart, ná eile.' It may have been that some language purists wanted it to remain that way and they may have thought that a translation would have made life a little simpler for the unfortunate students and teachers trying to make some sense of what Peig was telling them. On the other hand it may have been the opinion of others that a successful translation of the book could never be achieved.

In this interview (which we conducted in Irish) Mr Etchingham explains how he eventually chose and then persuaded Bryan MacMahon to attempt the translation, not without strong reluctance from Bryan. It was during a Writer's Week in

Listowel in the early 1970s that the plot was hatched by
Etchingham:

> Smaoinigh mé ar go leor, leor agus do chuas i gcomhar le mo
> chairde istigh ansin agus bhuel deiridís no, no, ná labhair leis siúd.
> Fiú, do luaigh mé Bryan McMahon agus dúirt siad no, tá Bryan ró-
> fhoclach. ... Writer's Week, théinn síos go Lios Tuathail ag buail-
> eadh le daoine macánta thíos an treo sin. Ach lá agus an rud sin
> ar m'intinn agam agus an t-aistriúchán ar m'intinn ... dúras le
> Bryan lá amháin tar amach go Trá Lí. Agus ní raibh fhios aige cad
> a bhí i gceist agamsa. Do thiomáin sé sin amach go Trá Lí agus
> leath slí amach an bóthar chur sé ceist orm cad é seo atá ar intinn
> agat. Do theastaigh uait ceist a chur orm, a dúirt sé. Sea, é seo,
> Bryan. Peig. Ó sea, Peig, bhí aithne mhaith agam ar Pheig, arsa
> seisean. Bhuaileas léi go minic. An gcuirfeá Béarla air? ... Bhí
> seisean ag tiomáint an charr. Do mhoilligh an carr. O, no, no, no,
> Ní fhéadfainn é sin a dhéanamh duit, a Chaoimhín. Ba mhaith
> liom cabhrú ar aon slí a fhéadfainn, ach tá an iomarca meas agam
> do Pheig, grá agam di, agus ní fhéadfainn smaoineamh ar Bhéarla
> a chur ar a cuid tuairimí pearsanta féinigh. Do leanamar ar
> aghaidh go Trá Lí. Do labhras leis arís tamaill do mhíosa ina
> dhiaidh agus, no, ní raibh sé ag teacht chugam ... Tar-éis aimsir
> bheag tháinig sé chugam agus dúirt sé, smaoinigh mé air agus
> d'aistrigh mé dhá chaibideal de, ar mhaith leat féachaint ar. Do
> sheol sé suas chugam é agus bhí sé go breá. Agus do lean an rud ar
> aghaidh mar sin. Agus fé mar a deirim do cuireadh amach é i 73.
> Agus ansin do bhí an t-aistriúchán, an eagrán Meiriceánach, cuir-
> eadh é sin amach i 74. Sin Syracuse University Press, New York.[25]

Having agreed to translate the book, Bryan MacMahon set
about his task, as was his custom, with great diligence. His
modus operandi, as described in his aforementioned address to
the University of Newfoundland was very thorough and painstaking:

Translation at best is a tricky business with numerous pitfalls for the unwary. Setting about the translation of Peig's autobiography into English in 1972–1973 I kept Peig's voice always in my ears, even to the extent of pausing at intervals to listen to it, before I began to translate a passage. So as to ground the translation on some reality, I also tried to imagine how Peig would have told her story had she been born on a small holding on the same Dingle peninsula, say twenty-five miles east of Dunquin where she and her people, though English-speaking, would have been only one generation removed from Irish as a vernacular.

For fifty years I have been informally studying the Kerry dialect of English, its cadences and its instinctive, aesthetic rectitude, as instanced say in the plays of George Fitzmaurice. In my writing room I first read aloud a chapter in the original Irish, marked dubious words and phrases, pondered on them, switched on the little microphone of the cassette recorder and, still mimicking Peig's voice, but in English this time, began to translate. The following day at school my typist did me a draft.

I was fortunate inasmuch as I could check the parochial meanings of certain words and phrases with Liam de Brún and Joe Daly. There are regional subtleties of dialect in Dunquin and the Blaskets that do not exist in Ballyferriter and Ballydavid, some miles to the north, where the areas have nuances of their own and where I had learned my Irish over a period of fifty years. To render Peig's poetry in Irish into poetry in English turned me into something like a worker in mosaic. The draft finished, I began the painstaking task of check and recheck on words, phrases and idioms.

The English edition of *Peig* was published by the Talbot Press in Dublin in 1973. Illustrations were provided by artist Caitriona O'Connor. We could not determine the actual publication date or the location. The launch may have taken place in the Peacock Theatre, according to Eibhlín Ní Mhurchú.

Few speakers of Irish impressed Bryan MacMahon more

than Eibhlín Ní Mhurchú, a mellifluous native of Baile Loisce in the west Kerry Gaeltacht, now an octogenarian living in Dublin. Her opinion of his translation would have pleased him no end:

> Is é seo an saghas Béarla a bheadh ag Peig, dá mbeadh sí ag labhairt Béarla.

In a foreword to the Syracuse University Press (1974) edition the late Eoin McKiernan, then president of the Irish American Cultural Institute, declared:[26]

> As layered, direct, and simple as the life it portrays, Bryan Mac-Mahon's translation from Peig's native Irish is an appropriate tribute to the great-souled woman and her people ...

The translator could not have done better than that.

The English translation of *Peig* was read on RTÉ Radio in 1983 and in an introduction to the readings the translator, Bryan MacMahon, had this to say:

> Peig is always close to the elemental forces of nature, of mating, of birth, and death. The islanders also lived close to clay, to air and breaking wave. Peig was rare insofar as she was a woman seanchaí, or traditional storyteller or entertainer if you like, a craft which she learned from her father. The craft of storytelling, which others have to take great pains to master and to learn, came to her, as the saying goes, by nature which cost no money at all.
>
> It's a quiet, gentle, midnight kind of book but nonetheless worthy for all that. Here in a landscape and seascape seen to effect in the film *Ryan's Daughter* Peig lived out her life on one of the last outposts of what can be loosely called a remnant of a Celtic empire.[27] The film fades in memory, but the memory of Peig and

her comrade writers lives on, as she herself puts it: 'People will yet walk in to the graveyard where I'll be lying but people like us will never again be there, we'll be stretched out quietly and the old world will have vanished.'

Since *Peig* was translated into English the book has been translated into French by Joelle Gac,[28] translated into German under the title *So Irisch wie Ich* (So Irish am I)[29] and partly translated into Dutch.

Not bad at all for an old lady from the Great Blasket.

1 Peig Sayers, *Peig* (Dublin: The Talbot Press, 1936).
2 For a general reference to St Brendan's life see the pamphlet produced by the Saint Brendan The Navigator Centre, Fenit (2004). Phone number 066/7136376.
3 The original of Othorna (Clanmaurice).
4 *Peig*, 1936.
5 Tomás Luibhéad (1904–80) was a teacher, author, playwright and Irish language activist who spent most of his adult life living in Dublin. See Breathnach and Ní Mhurchú, *Beathaisnéis A Trí, 1882–1982* (Dublin: An Clóchomhar, 2002).
6 This woman was not related to Peig Sayers of The Great Blasket according to Luibheád.
7 His address was published in Alison Feder and Bernice Schrank (eds), *Literature and Folk Culture: Ireland and Newfoundland, Papers from the Ninth Annual Seminar of the Canadian Association for Irish Studies at Memorial University of Newfoundland, February 11–15, 1976* (St John's, Newfoundland, Canada: Memorial University of Newfoundland, 1977).
8 *Here's Ireland* (London: B.T. Batsford Ltd, 1971).
9 Peig died in Dingle Hospital on 8 December 1958.

10 The interviewer was Seán Ó Cíobháin and the programme was initially broadcast on RnaG on 22 October 1987.

11 She ran Tigh Eibhlín with her husband, Paddy McWilliams, originally from Belfast.

12 Raconteur and founder of the famous Kruger's Pub in Dún Chaoin.

13 'Ceiliúradh an Bhlascaoid/The Great Blasket Commemoration: Filí agus Filíocht an Bhlascaoid/The Poets and Poetry of The Great Blasket', The Great Blasket Centre, 8–10 October 2004.

14 Seán Mac Réamoinn of Radio Éireann and others made recordings of her stories.

15 'Slán an Scéalaí/The Voice of Generations' produced and directed by Breandán Feiritéar, a native of Dún Chaoin, and originally broadcast on TG4 on 12 February 1998.

16 'Peig Sayers, Scéalaí/Peig Sayers, Storyteller' was the theme of Ceiliúradh an Bhlascaoid 3/The Blasket Commemoration 3, held in the Great Blasket Centre from 27–29 March 1998. The proceedings of An Ceiliúradh were published as *Ceiliúradh An Bhlascaoid 3* (Baile Átha Cliath: Coiscéim, 1999) under the editorial guidance of Máire Ní Chéilleachair.

17 Broadcast 15 January 2003 on RTÉ Radio 1 and produced by Cathal Póirtéir.

18 *Blasket Island Reflections*: a double CD and a special 52 page illustrated booklet was produced by Cathal Póirtéir for RTÉ and published on 17 November 2003, to mark the fiftieth anniversary of the official abandonment of the Great Blasket island.

19 Máire Ní Chinnéide (ed.), *Machtnamh Seanmhná* (Oifig an tSoláthair [Stationary Office], 1939).

20 *An Old Woman's Reflections*, translated from Irish by Séamus Ennis and introduced by W. R. Rodgers, published by Oxford University Press in 1962.

21 Edited by her son, Mícheal Ó Guithín, and published by Foilseacháin Náisiúnta Teoranta in 1970. Very few copies of this publication are available.

22 Published in 1928.

23 *An tOileánach* by Tomás Ó Criomhthain was first published in

Irish in 1929 by Muinntir C. S. Ó Fallamhain in co-operation with Oifig an tSoláthair. Translated into English by Robin Flower as *The Islandman* (Dublin: The Talbot Press and London: Chatto & Windus, 1937).

24 Published in Irish in 1933 by Clólucht an Talbóidigh, Tta. (Talbot Press) and translated into English by George Thomson and Moya Llewelyen Davies, with a foreword by E. M. Forster (London: Chatto & Windus, 1933).

25 *Peig, the autobiography of Peig Sayers of The Great Blasket island*, with illustrations by Caitriona O'Connor.

26 McKiernan died in summer 2004.

27 *Ryan's Daughter* was filmed by David Lean and MGM mostly in west Kerry in 1969.

28 *Peig, Autographie d'une grande conteuse d'Irlande* (An Here, 1999).

29 Peig Sayers, *So Irisch wie Ich, Eien Fischerfrau Erzähet ihr Leben* (Lamuv Göttingen, 1996).

CHAPTER EIGHT

Early Nineteenth-Century Education in North Kerry

Pádraig Ó Concubhair

Because the law forbade the teacher to teach he had to teach in secret; because the law forbade the farmer to shelter the school-master, he was forced to teach out of doors and he could only do this in suitable weather. So he looked for a remote spot and for the sunny side of a hedge or ditch, which would hide himself and his pupils from the passer-by and there he taught, seated on a stone while the pupils lay around him on the grass. One pupil was al-ways left on watch and should he spy strangers who might be informers or law officers he would at once warn the teacher. The class would be disbanded and the teacher with his books in his pocket would seize the spade or the hook and begin to work with a will.

This quotation from P. J. Dowling's *The Hedge Schools of Ireland* encapsulates the genesis of the 'Hedge Schools' and even though the rigorous implementation of the various penal laws against the education of Catholics was of short duration, in times of stress they were enforced. In May 1714, for example, Stephen Rice of Ballylougrhrin House in Lisselton parish, between Ballyduff and Ballybunion, was summoned before the justices in Tralee charged that 'he did send his son to France for learning'. At the same assizes 'Daniel Breen and Diarmuid (Darby) O'Connor, papish masters' were charged that 'they did teach youth in learning'. The masters did not appear in court. Stephen Rice did so. He would have been fined £20 with twelve months in jail if he had not.

By the first decades of the nineteenth century such happenings were but a memory. The successors of Daniel and Diarmuid were busily employed all over north Kerry. 'Pay schools', as the hedge schools were now called, were the only means by which most Catholics, and indeed some Protestants also, could obtain an education for their children.

The education they received in these schools depended solely on the capability of the master. The teaching was, of necessity, one to one, as it was the pupil's responsibility to provide the textbook. Three of the basic books in use were Gough's and Voster's *Arithmetics* and the *Ready my Daisy* – i.e. the 'Reading Made Easy' series. But many much more esoteric volumes were also to be found including, *The Life of Freney the Robber, Robin Hood, The Battle of Ventry Harbour, The Munster Farmer's Magazine* and *The Farmer's Daughter of Essex*.

Much was made of this variety of instructional manuals but there is no doubt that in the best instances of pay schools a superior quality of learning was imparted. As the Halls were to remark in 1841:

> It is by no means rare to find among the humblest of the peasantry of Kerry, who have no prospect of existing but that by daily labour, men who can converse fluently in Latin and have a good knowledge of Greek.

The same tradition is attested to in the collection of the Irish Folklore Commission:

Every pupil had a 'bittle' – a piece of wood planed about 5" by 12" and that's what they put their copies on. They wrote regular copper-plate on it even though they might get a nudge from the next scholar now and then. Jack Gunne was a schoolmaster in Lisselton and his brother Dick must have been to school to him for he used to say 'Lauda (recte Oda) profanis vulgis,' that is, 'keep at arm's length from the profane order.'

Mickey Moriarty from Dingle side was a hedge teacher in Dooncaha (Tarbert Parish) and he educated the Creaghs and the De Courcys and the Ellliots. (The families of the local gentry.) Pat Lane taught in Dooncaha. When the National Schools were established the parish priest wanted to have Lane as a teacher in Tarbert. He was working in a bog when the inspector came to examine him stripped down to his flannel drawers. His appearance came against him. The inspector began to examine him in Euclid. 'Wait, now,' he said and he ran into the house and brought out a griddle and he made the inspector look foolish for he couldn't answer the problems he drew in the griddle.

When British government policy towards Ireland moved away from the principle 'Cuius Regio Eis Religio', i.e. that the religion of the people should be the state religion, a principle that, unfortunately from their perspective, the Irish were most unwilling to adopt – their new ideal was summed up in the words of Archbishop Boulter of the Established (Church of Ireland) Church. He wrote: 'To bring the nation over to true religion, one of the likeliest methods we can think of, is, if possible, the instructing and converting of the younger generation.' As we shall see this principle was to lead to the setting up of a system of education parallel to that of the pay schools and the tension thus established was one of the reasons for setting up the national school system in the third decade of the nineteenth century.

However by 1812 a parliamentary committee had laid down the axiom that popular education in Ireland should be conducted without any attempt to interfere with the doctrines of different religious persuasions and it recognised that the majority of the people were Catholic and likely to remain so. But this principle, even when accepted, also led to difficulties. The schools to which the state gave assistance still enjoined daily Bible study and, as the Catholic authorities objected to the unrestricted reading of the Bible, the setting up of a mass educational system could not be achieved. As the noted educationalist Richard Lowell Edgeworth wrote at the time:

> There are persons who think that allowing Catholic Bishops and Catholic Clergy to have any share in the superintendence of schools is unsafe and a degradation of the dignity of protestant Clergymen to act along with them. How this opinion can be made consistent with the clerical character or with that Christian charity for which all ministers of the gospel ought to be distinguished. It can never be good policy to degrade the ministers of the church in the eyes of the people whose consciences they direct and whose morals they are to form.

In 1824 then, the government called on the 'five wise men', Thomas F. Lewis, John Leslie Foster, William Grant, James Glassford and Anthony R. Blake:

> To inquire into the nature and extent of the instruction afforded by the schools of Ireland and to report as to what measures could be adopted to extend generally to all the people of Ireland the benefits of Education.

As this was forty-eight years before a national system of education was set up in England and Wales we might be inclined to applaud this enlightened thinking on behalf of the people of Ireland were it not for the fact that the same John Leslie Foster said that:

> A more disloyal and bigoted set of men does not exist than the Hedge-Schoolmasters of Ireland – those incapable of gaining a livelihood by any other means are constrained to open a school as a last resource.

Though the British government had come to realise that the Catholics of Ireland were liable to remain Catholics and within five years were to recognise their official existence by the granting of Catholic emancipation, it was hoped that the result of the new education system would be that summed up in John Hullah's lines:

> I thank the goodness and the grace
> That on my birth have smiled,
> And made me in these Christian days
> A happy English child.

The opening decades of the nineteenth century were a time of turmoil in Ireland and particularly in Kerry. The threat of organised political revolt as exemplified in 1798 and 1803 had been faced down and the restoration of the monarchy and the death of Bonaparte had seemed to signal the end of political activity. Instead, groups of men roamed the countryside at night wearing white shirts as a uniform. They fought against the exorbitant rents imposed by landlords and their agents and against the tithe charge of the Established Church. They also tried to regulate the dues paid to the Catholic priests. Hay ricks and corn stacks were burned, cattle and horses were houghed or lamed and sometimes driven over cliffs. Agents and tithe-collectors were whipped or had their flesh torn with iron combs or were buried in pits of thorns.

As William Carleton wrote:

> The young men of a locality stood in need of some person who might regulate their proceedings, keep their memberships lists, appoint their meetings and preside over them and organise their activities with skill and precision.
>
> Who was better able to do this than the local schoolteacher?

The parliamentary commission of 1824 conducted a survey of the state of schools of Ireland. A questionnaire was sent to rectors and parish priests. From the answers to this we learn that in the nine civil parishes north of the Feale there were thirty-three schools, twenty-six of which were pay schools.

These represented three-quarters of the educational establishments of north Kerry. What of the other schools? These, to a greater or lesser extent, either sprang from the ideals of Primate Boulter a half century before or were set up as a reaction to schools thus founded. The returns for north Kerry almost replicated the national figures. In Ireland there were 9,352 pay schools. There were 919 schools affiliated to the Society for the Promotion of the Education of the Poor of Ireland – commonly called the Kildare Place Society, and almost the same number connected with groups such as the Society for the Promotion of the Knowledge and Practice of the Christian Religion, the Erasmus Smith Trust, the London Hibernian Society, the Irish Society and the Baptist and Methodist Missionary Schools. All these, with the exception of the Kildare Place Society, had as an overt object the saving of souls by converting children and, it was hoped, their parents, from the Catholic faith.

But it was not these schools that were the problem as, *ipso facto*, they were hardly likely to propagate treason. The pay schools on the other hand had to be dealt with. That this might be done Lord Stanley, then chief secretary, the government minister responsible for Ireland, wrote his famous letter to the Duke of Leinster, inviting him to become chairman:

> Of a Board of Commissioners of Education, who should establish a system of combined literary and separate religious instruction, which should be so far adapted to the religious persuasions which prevail in Ireland as to render it in truth, a system of national education for the country.

The commissioners would make grants of two-thirds of the cost towards the erection of schoolhouses and they would augment the salary the teachers received from local funds. But since there generally were no local funds they soon found themselves paying the entire salary. They would provide inspectors and a training system for teachers and they would edit and print schoolbooks and supply these and other requisites at half price.

The opportunity was too good to miss and, just as in 1798, the Presbyterians took the lead. The first school in Ireland to be registered was in Glenarriffe, near Cushendall in County Antrim. The roll number was 001, the teacher was George Doran and the manager was E. O'Neill. In fact most of the early schools to join the national system were from the province of Ulster.

The first application to establish a school in Kerry came from Dingle from Rev. Mr O'Sullivan, PP, Rev. G. Naughton and prominent lay members of the Established Church (the Church of Ireland). It was necessary to have signatories of both Catholic and Protestants to obtain favourable consideration for an application for a school but the vast majority of Church of Ireland ministers resolutely opposed the new system as it allowed no reading of the Bible during secular hours of teaching. The Church proceeded to establish its own organisation for primary schools, the Church Education Society, subsuming the Kildare Place Society which no longer obtained grants from the government. In effect this lasted until the Church of Ireland was disestablished in 1869 and indeed thereafter it continued to give grants to help the educational needs of Church of Ireland children. Over the years, however, the cost of supporting a separate educational system became too much for the Church and their schools joined the national system. The last relic of the societies lasted into our own time until the government made the Church of Ireland College of Education an offer it could not refuse and it vacated its site at Kildare Place and relocated to Rathmines.

Though the first applications to become part of the new system came mainly from Ulster, Kerry was not far behind. Moyvane had been the site of one of the seven free schools in north Kerry in 1824. This was thanks to the landlord, John Leslie Foster. He had come into possession of the lands of 'Meevane' in 1811 and, with his agent Michael Enright, he founded a school there in 1818 under the aegis of the Kildare Place Society. It was described as 'a good house, 50 feet long 16 feet wide with four windows and a thatched roof, fit for 150 children'. It was also 'well furnished with seats and desks after the model of Phillipstown, Co Louth'.

A new house was also built for the master, Michael Keane, and by the time all was paid for, including a library of eighty books which counted amongst its number *Robinson Crusoe* and *Aesop's Fables*, Mr Foster had spent well over £50. Michael became the first Kerry teacher to be trained by the society. The training lasted for six weeks. 'This was ample to prevent the teachers becoming socially superior to the pupils and getting ideas above their station.'

Six weeks may not have been enough for Michael for, in 1825, the inspector described him as 'being among the very worst teachers I have seen'. By the end of the 1820s Baron Foster seemed to tire of his school in Moyvane and the parish priest took it over in 1827. He applied for inclusion in the national system in 1833 and the roll number was 532. When the commissioners' inspector visited the school in 1835 he found ninety boys and forty-seven girls present. Michael had been joined by his wife Jane and the inspector reported that: 'the school was in ruins for the want of thatching, the windows were broken, the desks were rotting and both teachers were decidedly bad!'

The problem of repairs was solved when on the 'Night of the Big Wind', 6 January 1839, the school was 'almost entirely tumbled'. Michael reopened it in his own house, and when the inspector said this was not suitable he removed to the chapel where he remained until the new school was built.

In this he was only keeping up the traditions of the pay schools: at the time of the 1824 survey, John Donoghue was teaching one hundred and twenty children in Gunsboro' chapel in the parish of Galey (Ballydonoghue); Michael Rooney taught ninety children in the chapel at Gortnaskeha in the parish of Killaheny (Ballybunion); Patrick Quinn was responsible for eighty-eight scholars in the chapel at Cockhill in Kilnaughtin (Tarbert) parish. In the Folklore Commission records we find the following account in confirmation of this:

In them days the chapels were ordinary mud walled cabins and they were used as schools and farmers used thresh corn in them and carpenters make carts in them. The carpenters had one side of the house to themselves and the scholars the other side.

Father McCarthy, parish priest of the united parishes of Bally-longford and Tarbert also favoured the national system but for a different reason. In his view, the Kildare place school at Sal-lowglin on the borders of the two parishes was used as a proselytising school by the manager, Thomas Sandes, in contradiction of the society's rules. He had forbidden his parishioners to attend the school and this led to an incident in Ballylongford chapel which was reported by the *Kerry Evening Post*, the local unionist newspaper:

An honest and industrious tradesman from Ballylongford is bearing on his head the horrors of priestly excommunication. The head and front of this poor man's crime is that he persists in sending his children to the Sallowglin Free School, which we have the best authority for saying, that there is not a better conducted school or one so well attended to in any part of the kingdom. The Scriptures of truth, however, are used there by such children as are able to read them fluently – Hinc illae Lacryimae – Hence the opposition from those who style themselves as ministers of the Gospel. *The Chevalier de Faubais, the Life of Captain Feeny, the Robber, Moll Flanders* and *Dangerous Connexions* are admissable into schools strictly Roman Catholic, when the pure and holy word of God is excluded.

The dismayed mechanic, ventured to remonstrate with the priest and entreated that he 'would not judge him'. His Reverance, indignant at any thing bordering on opposition, flung off his robes and threatened to kick him out. The poor man unwilling to afford this minister of peace an opportunity to: 'Prove his doctrine orthodox by apostolic blows and hard knocks' wisely quitted the chapel, the door of which was ordered to be closed after him.

Father McCarthy applied for permission to build in Ballylongford and Tarbert in 1833 and it seems the buildings were completed within a year. The school building in Tarbert is still to be seen and has been tastefully renovated as a community hall. The inspector arrived in Ballylongford on 17 August 1835, but he refused to enter the school because of an 'objectionable inscription' he found on the building which read: 'Ballylongford National Schools, Rev. D. McCarthy, R.C. Rector.' By 12 December Father McCarthy reported that the inscription had been removed and a more suitable one substituted. In due course a grant was paid to build that most vital of features, 'the boundary wall', once famously coupled by an inspector with the pupils in the Third Book of Lessons: 'both weak in composition'. Further grants followed for building privies, furnishing the house, painting the doors and window sashes and providing flooring and grates.

As in many schools at the time, maintenance was non-existent and by 1853, the schools were in a 'most dilapidated state'. A letter was sent to the trustees threatening legal proceedings in the hope that it 'might be productive of good effect and rendered further proceedings unnecessary'. No answer was received from Father McCarthy, but the letter to the other trustee, Pierce Crosbie of Rusheen House, was returned marked 'dead'. Salary was withdrawn from the teachers on 1 July 1854. This galvanised Father McCarthy into action and repairs were completed to the inspector's satisfaction by 18 August.

Glin, Co. Limerick, was described in the state papers at the time of the 1798 Rebellion as the 'centre of sedition'. It seems that Tarbert, some forty years later could be said to be a 'centre of learning'. According to a report drawn up by the British methodist conference on 'Wesleyan Missions in the Heathen Countries'(!) it contained:

> An infant school, a very good national school for boys and girls, a school maintained by the foundation of Erasmus Smith (a gentleman who died many years since and left property sufficient to provide for one hundred good daily schools and four classical schools all connected with the Established Church [of Ireland]), a classical school, if it may be called such, for the writer found the boys, when he visited it, reading Virgil, etc., sitting on large blocks of wood for want of seats in a very poor hut. The county of Kerry is famous for poor lads learning the classics.
>
> There are other private schools and the Wesleyan Mission school which takes precedence over all the rest as it was begun in the year 1826. There are 24 boys and 11 girls there – 8 in the alphabet class, 12, spelling, 15 reading in the New Testament and 10 in the Bible class and of these 20 write, cipher and learn the (Methodist) Conference Catechism.'

Ballylongford and Tarbert were followed by other parishes. On the eve of the Great Famine, there were 3,637 national schools in Ireland and ninety-nine of these were in Kerry. Of the ninety-nine, four were in the parish of Duagh, five in Rattoo, five in Killury, four in Listowel including one in the workhouse, two in Kilmoiley, one in Asdee, one in Lisselton and of course, Michael Keane still taught in Moyvane. That these thirty-odd schools were quite effective can be seen by the returns from Listowel workhouse in 1849 of those who could read and write in the age groups which had been exposed to the new system. One by one the 'pay-schools' died out. In many cases the masters took service under the commissioners of education, trading off the freedom of choosing their own curriculum against the certainty of a quarterly salary. The epitaph of the 'poor scholar' was heard no more:

> Here I lie at the church door,
> Here I lie because I'm poor,
> The farther in the more they pay,
> And here I lie, as warm as they.

Instead, scholars crowded into the schools to receive the food and clothing provided by the British Association for the Relief of Famine in Ireland. This kept many alive who would otherwise have added to the multitudes who perished. However they had to undergo the conditions described by an inspector at the time:

Who does not remember the comparative freshness and vigour of mind and body with which the morning's recitations were begun and the languor and weariness of body, the confusion of mind, the dry skin, the flushed cheek, the aching head, the sickening sensation, the unnatural demand for drink, the thousand excuses to get out of door, which came along in quick succession as the day advanced and especially on a winter's afternoon, when the overheated and un-renewed atmosphere had become obvious to every sense? These were nature's signals of distress and who can forget the delicious sensations with which her balmy breath, when admitted on the occasional opening of the door would visit the brow and the face and be felt all along the revitalised blood, or the newness of life, with which every nerve muscle and mind were endured by free exercise in the open air at recess and the close of the school.

And that was just the Master! How must the poor children have felt?

CHAPTER NINE

'Skill'd to Rule': the Teacher and Irish Literature

Mary Shine Thompson

Oliver Goldsmith's village schoolmaster in *The Deserted Village* (1770) is often presented affectionately as the prototype of the perfect traditional schoolmaster. He is kind, numerate, literate, and infinitely more learned than the rustics that range round him. The skills he possesses – his ability to measure land and predict tides, for instance – are practical and useful. On further investigation, however, we discover him to be severe and given to what we might now call mood swings. ('Well had the boding tremblers learn'd to trace/The day's disasters in his morning face'.) In their own interests, his pupils humour him by laughing, but 'with counterfeited glee,/At all his jokes'. He seems to have mastered the art of rhetoric, but to what end? 'E'en though vanquish'd, he could argue still.' One might well ask whether an incisive intelligence would continue to argue 'e'en though vanquish'd'! And while the speaker of Goldsmith's verse affects to adopt a naïve voice, wondrous that 'one small head could carry all he knew', we can detect a certain scepticism, an irony of tone that actually punctures arrogant assumptions about the superiority of apparently learned folk. The last lines remind us of the teacher's fame and his triumphs rather than his learning: 'But past is all his fame. The very spot/Where many a time he

triumphed is forgot.' The Irish have always loved to shy coco-
nuts at those they place on pedestals. Perhaps this verse is an
example of sly satire on the follies of pride in a little learning.

The theme of the inspirational teacher has been more
popular in cinema than in Irish literature: witness *To Sir with
Love* (1967), *Stand and Deliver* (1988), *Lean on Me* and *Dead
Poets Society* (both 1989) and *Dangerous Minds* (1995). Despite
the high regard in which individual teachers have been held in
their local communities – and indeed their sterling contributions to the same communities – it is relatively rare for teachers
to come well out of twentieth-century Irish adult literature or
official reports. From the 1830s, the commissioners for national
education in Ireland commented regularly on the 'ignorance' of
teachers, both those in hedge schools and in the newly-estab-
lished national schools. An account by William Carleton, who
himself had spent time as both a pupil and a teacher in a hedge
school, embroiders on the motif of Goldsmith's village schoolmaster in 'The Hedge School' from *Traits and Stories of the Irish
Peasantry* (1830). It tells of a teacher who ostentatiously displays his pedantry. Brian Friel's verbose hedge schoolmaster in
Translations (1981) and the master in *Philadelphia, Here I Come!*
(1965) set in the 1960s, are in the same mould. Both are given
to the drink and to uttering grandiose promises, while neither
delivers a great deal. However, we do well to recall that there
is considerable evidence in, for example, P. J. Dowling's *Hedge
Schools of Ireland* (1935) that some hedge schoolmasters pro-
moted outstanding standards of scholarship. Indeed, Carleton
himself noted the literary knowledge of the hedge schoolmasters was superior to those of the national school teachers who
replaced them: 'young men educated in Irish hedge schools ...
have proved themselves to be better classical scholars and

mathematicians, generally speaking, than any proportionate number of those educated in our first-rate academies. The Munster masters have long been, and still are, particularly celebrated for making excellent classical and mathematical scholars.'

Teaching as a profession in Ireland has been a highly-regarded career option throughout the twentieth century. For decades primary school teaching has attracted students from the top quartile of the leaving certificate examination, students of the highest acumen. Recent OECD reports have commented on the link between Ireland's educational system and the country's remarkable economic success. This makes the gap between the literary representations of teachers and reality even more interesting.

Perhaps the most disturbing recent portraits of Irish teachers are to be found in Patrick McCabe's novel, *The Dead School* (1995). It is not the depiction of the clearly psychotic central protagonist Malachy Dudgeon, a primary teacher who recedes into a solipsistic twilight as the story unfolds, that is most troubling: after all, the mad cruelty of one man hardly condemns a whole profession. Rather, it is the utter dreariness and casual cruelty of his teaching colleagues that is so damning. The impact on the reader is heightened by the ease and verisimilitude of McCabe's evocation of the rhythms and rituals of the school day and the mindset it can engender. The principal teacher, Raphael Bell, the great deadener, sets the tone with his piety and petty obsessions, and Mr Boylan glares like someone possessed when Malachy innocently uses his teacup. This pair epitomises mindless power mongering, and the inane staff-room conversation confirms that this is indeed a dead school. Pity the pupils.

That some teachers of the twentieth century failed to ignite intellectual passions may have to do with the Irish penchant for what the historian Joe Lee has called the possession ethic. In the first four decades of the new Irish state, a period bedevilled by emigration, Irish society recognised the value of education insofar as it led to secure, pensionable employment such as teaching. Some teachers, however, having achieved the glittering monarchy of a classroom, came to see their kingdom as restrictive and limited, a prison both for them and their pupils. A little education was dangerous to the less able and creative teachers, setting them apart from their neighbours. Being set apart, a great deal of power in the small dominion of the classroom made demigods out of the least happy of them. We know from recent tribunal evidence and from Mary Raftery and Eoin O'Sullivan's *Suffer Little Children* (1999), that there was widespread tolerance of brutality in Ireland in the early and mid-twentieth century. In this respect teachers were probably no better or no worse than their contemporaries. For every portrait of a barbarous or sadistic teacher, there is another of a heartless father: I don't think I have ever introduced John McGahern's novels or short-stories in the lecture hall without students commenting on how familiar was the cruelty of his fictitious fathers.

Given human nature, it is inevitable that many teachers fall short of Olympian heights. However, their negative portraiture in literature, especially in autobiographical tales, cannot be ascribed solely to their personal limitations. I use 'tale' advisedly: autobiography is dependent on memory that is, as we know, arbitrary in its operation and often unreliable as evidence. The motives that cause the tale to be spun in the first place and then drive it to be published are complex and not easily unravelled. The story of a life is the record of an individual's struggles to displace the received order of the world to make space for him or herself. Authority, however configured, must be challenged, and the greater the struggle, the more momentous the achievement of the autobiographer. So, overcoming a hard start may be an early measure of the heroic resilience of the writer.

Other factors may complicate the unvarnished truth that autobiographical tales of hardship in school purport to convey. A teacher provides a child with the first experience of public modes of authority, and in so doing imposes restrictions necessary to public life. A degree of formality and regulation, which a child might interpret as coldness if contrasted with the comfort and ease of home, is necessary in school. There, large numbers of children must not only coexist, but also be acculturated into formal ways of being in the world. This process pits the individual against the teacher. Incidents that highlight the teacher's cruelty encapsulate the challenge facing the individual struggling for ascendancy or autonomy in the world. The central point about many episodes of classroom conflicts is that they crystallise key moments that advance the story and highlight the individual's progress towards self-determination.

The larger the number of children and the more impoverished the classrooms, the greater the strain on all, so pressurising the less competent teacher into taking shortcuts with justice. Imagine, for example, what strain there must have been on the infant teacher who was also Bryan MacMahon's mother! In his book, *The Master* (1992), he comments, as it were in passing, that she had an incredible 120 infants in her class. (I can attest from experience to the fact that even in the 1970s half that number was not unusual in some classes.) Even with superhuman skills, the efforts to juggle curricula, discipline and crowd control could lead to hasty, ill-conceived and unjust treatment.

Two poems by contemporary poets indicate how classroom discipline becomes a metaphor for the perversion, self-delusion and cruelty of state ideology, as transmitted by teachers in state schools. In Paul Muldoon's 'Anseo', we meet the young Joseph Mary Plunkett Ward, whom the master sends out to the hedge-rows to find a stick with which he will be beaten. He learns the lessons of the discipline only too well, and grows up to live on a secret camp, where he trains volunteers to fight 'for Ireland'. John Montague's 'A Grafted Tongue' harks back to a time when marks were gouged on a tally-stick every time a child in a national school spoke Irish, so driving a wedge between Irish-speaking parents and their children. Montague points to the humiliation inherent in growing 'a grafted tongue', and to the irony of children now stumbling as they struggle to learn what is an official language of the state. These poems suggest that political imperialism not only governs institutions of learning, but entire fields of study and even the imagination. Their un-derlying message has its antecedent in the famous passage in James Joyce's *A Portrait of the Artist as a Young Man* (1914), in which the young Stephen Dedalus engages with the dean of studies, an Englishman in Stephen's school, on the use of the word 'tundish'. The dean is a limited, literal-minded man, un-familiar with the term: to him the vessel in question is a funnel. Dedalus, the precocious Irish student, is therefore placed in the awkward position of the colonial subject who is obliged to in-struct the coloniser on the use of his own language. He realises that the dean's language will always remain foreign to him. It will always be a familiar tongue that has been acquired but not accepted. However, as a boy in the presence of a teacher, he lacks the necessary authority, either cultural or in terms of status, to teach the teacher. What matters in this episode is symbolic authority over knowledge that the colonised subject is denied.

The tundish incident – and the other instances cited above – raise issues about the legitimacy of the authority of which the teacher is a conduit. Parents, while they accept a teacher's authority by virtue of placing their children in schools, regularly question that authority. One such is Mary Barber (c.1690–1757), wife of an English woollen-draper living in Dublin, and an acquaintance of Jonathan Swift, who began writing poetry to buoy up her children's lessons. She writes an excuse addressed to her son's master, explaining why he has not written his exercise on coronation day: 'Why are we Scholars plagu'd to write,/On Days devoted to Delight?/In Honour of the KING, I'd play/Upon his Coronation Day.' She playfully berates the teacher for encouraging poetry: 'I sent you to Latin, he makes you a Poet:/A fine way of training a Shopkeeper's Son!/'Twould better become him to teach you to dun [that is, to press for payment of a debt].' When the boy is commanded to write some verse on the death of an unnamed lord, she takes no nonsense: 'My Mother says, if e'er she hears/I write again of worthless Peers,/Whether they're living Lords, or dead,/She'll box the Muse from out my head.'

It would be a mistake to assume that all teachers represented in Irish literature lack insight into their various predicaments (as does Joyce's dean of studies) or that they are, like Patrick McCabe's Malachy Dudgeon, certifiable or criminal. The blistering honesty and clear vision of the teacher in John McGahern's *The Leavetaking* (1974), who shivers at the prospect of withering into his pension, of repeating the same patterns year in, year out, distances him from his counterparts. Dónal Foley in *Three Villages* has a brief sketch of a teacher working ceaselessly to ensure that his working-class pupils understand the practical applications of simultaneous equations, teaching his simple-interest lesson, for example, by reference to the pawnshop's profit from the weekly traffic in suits. Foley's report stresses the high esteem in which the teacher is held, and the writer's own affection for the man who, it transpires, is his father. Frank McCourt's *'Tis* (1999), his second volume of autobiography which covers his teaching career in New York, shows how he wins over his disaffected teenagers who yawningly dismiss the prescribed classics as 'dumb books'. So McCourt surreptitiously introduces them to *The Catcher in the Rye* (1951) – it's not sanctioned and he must do so without permission – and the youngsters recognise something of their lives and their hostility in it. Following complaints from parents, the only book the youngsters have ever actually read is removed. It is to McCourt's credit that Shakespeare takes the teenagers' fancy: the bard is not sanctioned either, but somehow McCourt gets away with that. Passionate discussion ensues as to why Ophelia didn't leave for America rather than opt for the river. (The students establish that there was an America in Shakespeare's time and 'she cudda went'.) Of course, self-promotion is part of American culture, but even making judicious allowance for this, McCourt conveys success similar to that of the fictional teacher in *To Sir With Love* who manages to imbue disenchanted teenagers with some enthusiasm for school.

Kate O'Brien's novel *The Land of Spices* (1941), a reflection on a girl's schooling, is exceptional in its subject matter and its depth: it contains more than one complex portrayal of a teacher. There is, for example, Mother Mary Andrew, whose unjust treatment of the school baby, Anna (she reduces her marks in a grammar test from a creditable seventy-five to zero because of one error), causes great upheaval. Reverend Mother, a woman confident of her authority, censures her, by implication supporting a pupil against a teacher – unheard of behaviour. This incident from the beginning of the book finds its echo at the end, when Reverend Mother challenges the assumption by Anna's grandmother that the girl should find work in a bank rather than pursue an academic career. Despite her moralising, Reverend Mother is not slow to use all the weapons in her armoury to have her way: she threatens the law on the respectable grandmother, Mrs Condon, if she withdraws Anna's fees, and warns that she can destroy the career of Mrs Condon's clerical brother. It becomes clear that the two women are sisters under the skin: both understand how to deploy power with the assurance of their class, and they differ from the teachers already identified in the degree, rather than the nature, of their power.

Power mongering takes even more sinister turns in some Irish autobiographical and fictional classrooms. Their monarchs strut and swagger, their peacock displays of power often crossing the border to lunacy. In Muiris Ó Suileabháin's *Twenty Years a-Growing* (1933), for instance, the schoolmistress is probably guilty of an indictable offence, in that she ties the errant children to a post. The evil genius of Miss Killeen presides over Mary Beckett's semi-autobiographical novel *Give Them Stones* (1987). Like other teachers we encounter in adult fiction, she lacks a sense of proportion: when a box of biscuits, intended as a raffle prize, is accidentally knocked to the ground, she grabs a child at random and beats her black and blue. Beckett is at pains to make the point that the children continue to bring their pennies so that Miss Killeen can buy maps that will win her the coveted Carlisle and Blake Memorial Prize for teaching excellence.

Teachers' obsessions with certain aspects of the curriculum often reflect their own control phobias. The devotion of Seán Ó Faoláin's Christian Brother teacher, Sloppy Dan (in *Vive Moi!*, 1964) to the complex and unyielding discipline of English grammar finds its correlative in his punishment strap. However, it is the evocation of the physical presence of the manic sadist with his purple face, bulging eyes and bellowing mouth that still breathes terror into the reader. The dread was not only of the physical consequences of perceived misdemeanours: Breandán Ó hEithir claims in *Over the Bar* (1984) that his teacher invented the concept of thought police before George Orwell. In conveying a teacher's sustained sarcasm and disgust at a pupil's poor academic performance – a pupil, who, it transpires, ironically, is about to take up a position as a monitor, a trainee teacher – the example of Mr Monaghan in Hugh McVeigh's *Oft in the Stilly Night* has few equals. Frank O'Connor's more light-hearted but no less serious *An Only Child* notes in passing that when the eponymous child aped the 'simple manly' public-schoolboy behaviour that he found in comics, his teachers interpreted his initiative as an impertinence. Maura Laverty's autobiography *Never No More* describes how she endured misery in school after she offered a spontaneous remark that contradicted the teacher. The power-greedy crave total submission, it seems.

If McCabe's teachers are the most disheartening, Joyce's are probably the most famous. In *A Portrait of the Artist as a Young Man* the young Stephen Dedalus, a boarder in Clongowes

Wood College, breaks his glasses, and is exempted from study by Father Arnall. Despite this exemption, the prefect of studies, Father Dolan, accuses him of idling and whips him with his pandybat. Stephen, along with his young classmates, believes his punishment undeserved, and his fellow schoolboys cheer when he complains to the rector about the incident. The rector concedes that a mistake has been made, and, stretching his hand out to Stephen, implicitly acknowledges their equal status in the matter. This is a key incident on the road to Stephen's artistic priesthood, as it marks the moment when he refuses to conform to the will of his teachers, and, since they are also priests, to the authority of the Church.

The perspective of the teacher-narrator inevitably differs from that of the pupil, as Bryan MacMahon's *The Master* (1992) demonstrates. A teacher who went from the slums of Dublin to the urban poverty of Listowel, he was imbued with the vision of post-independence Ireland – a vision of a Gaelic Ireland that withered for many of his peers in emigration and drudgery. His *saevo indignatio* at the primitive and insanitary conditions in which his pupils are expected to learn is palpable. His is an outrage that identifies him as the dependable and commanding spokesman for his reticent pupils. Yet there is no sentimentalism, no attempt to conceal his own shortcomings, and he admits to his frustrations, lashing out on one occasion: 'I would rather be piking dung than teaching you fellows!' His teaching methods are orthodox: 'I had to lead, drive or coax [the pupils] along the harsh road to knowledge.' He has clear views on teaching methodology, and is analytical in his approach to his profession (or is it an art or a craft?) – identifying humour, love of learning, and a sense of wonder as essentials. He takes pleasure in articulating his methods, some of which,

such as paired reading, are now considered innovative. He dis-
approves of abstractions and the rigidity of his faith. If Mac-
Mahon's approach to teaching were to be described in the par-
lance of contemporary teaching studies, it would be situated
somewhere along a continuum between a teacher- and student-
centred model, in which the teacher is perceived as an expert,
the embodiment of formal authority, but also as a facilitator
and a personal model for the children. Such an educator encourages children to observe processes as well as content, and
also designs activities, social interactions and problem-solving
situations, so enabling the children not only to accumulate
deposits of knowledge, but, more importantly, to practise the
processes by which that knowledge is acquired.

MacMahon admits to having a strong authoritarian streak
('I could not afford to be defied'), betraying its extent in his use
of a military metaphor: 'A teacher, like an army, must always
have some line of retreat.' His observation that 'a good teacher
leaves the print of his teeth on a parish for three generations' is
also a somewhat disconcerting metaphor, implying as it does
the image of a hunter playing with its prey. But he has sufficient
self-knowledge to recognise that he suffers some degree of in-
security about his authority. The pride he takes in work well
done is honest and merited, but perhaps also tainted with a
streak of egocentrism; for instance, he records the success of a
former pupil who secured 'a good job with the Bell Company'
and is still 'on my way up' as due to the fact that the master
taught him his tables.

Implicit in MacMahon's attitude is the assumption that his
authority as a teacher is right, lawful and equitable. He himself
was ready to question authority when he believed it unjust –
the fact that he chose to write regularly for the periodical *The*

Bell at a time when ecclesiastical authorities viewed with suspicion its anti-censorship stance is evidence of this (and of his independence of spirit). So is his readiness to confront clerical school managers about the appalling condition of schools, and to berate the then Minister for Education, Dick Mulcahy, former IRA chief-of-staff and GOC of the defence forces: 'the inheritors of your revolution were rewarded with squalor.' His reservations about authority superior to his own are manifest in anecdotes about teachers jousting with schools inspectors, representatives of the Department of Education and often former teachers themselves. He also condones his pupils tickling trout and salmon in restricted stretches of the river, defending them by appeal to higher authority divined by himself: 'the fish bear no owner's brand'. Above all, however, it is enthusiasm and commitment that distinguish MacMahon's apologia for teaching. His book neatly defines the gap between a teacher's perception of the world of school and that of a former pupil who writes about it as an adult.

We may well ask whether the pattern of predominantly negative depictions of teachers to be found in adult tales is evident in books for children also. I have drawn heavily so far on autobiographical fiction and memoirs, since it is in these that teachers most often appear. This is not a category that has provided children with a great deal of reading matter, but one exception is Peig Sayers' *Peig* (1936, translated by MacMahon in 1973), which was a prescribed text in Irish secondary schools for generations. In a conforming, traditional tale such as this – and by 'traditional' in this context I mean a tale that affirms authoritarian, traditional relationships between adults and children – we encounter in passing Peig's teachers. The *maistreás* is romanticised, reinvented as the object of the male gaze, to use the terminology of feminist critics. The *máistir* is cast in the mould of MacMahon himself (he is a kindly man) and Peig accepts his authority without question. It is worth noting that he speaks in English to his exclusively Irish-speaking audience; this does not in any way make him the focus of the community's resentment.

Seamus Deane's *Reading in the Dark* (1996), now a text favoured in secondary schools, includes a chapter that offers insight into approaches to teaching in boys' secondary schools in the 1950s. The book evokes a mathematics class in which a clerical teacher, Father Gildea, employs a Socratic method that has degenerated into a sophists' game as a means of supervising the class as it corrects its homework. When Socrates employed the method, he began by professing ignorance of the subject in question, and this is the base from which students launch their pursuit of knowledge. He would then typically subject a hastily-formed opinion to probing scrutiny, in order that a more refined concept might be articulated. This would lead the interlocutor to find correct definitions, that are tested by reference to common experiences, and their implications are then drawn out. The class in Deane's book is well versed in the method, captured in this exchange:

> 'Are you more literate or more numerate as a consequence of my loving care, five times a week, forty minutes per time, McConnellogue?'
>> 'I am equally blessed in both respects, Father.'
>> 'Would you say that McConnellogue will go far, Heaney?'
>> 'I would, Father.'
>> 'Under what conditions would you say so, Heaney?'
>> 'Under the conditions imposed by the question, Father.'
>> 'Are you conversant with the conditions, Duffy?'

'I am, Father.'

'What's your name, Duffy?'

'Duffy, Father.'

While the method itself is formally elegant, here in the hands of its abuser it is marked by a deep cynicism, a definitive and haughty scepticism. Here the unscrupulous Father Gildea models for his pupils a means of manipulating facts in order to arrive at a foregone conclusion – in this case their failure to outwit the sophist-teacher and, as a consequence, the doubling of homework for the whole class. The episode acts as a cautionary tale that illustrates how the narrator and his peers struggle to make sense of the world – to read it in a dark further dimmed by those ostensibly in the business of enlightening them.

More often than not, however, teachers figure only in a shadowy way in children's books (and then mostly in realist fiction for older children), and their characters are rarely well developed. This is the case in Carlo Gébler's *Frozen Out: A Tale of Betrayal and Survival* (1998), which is about an English family that comes to settles in Northern Ireland. A cardboard-thin teacher presides over a sketchily-drawn school in an otherwise interesting story about the problems of integration in a new community. It is sobering to see just how peripheral school and teachers are to the imaginative and the real lives of children, despite the fact that they spend such a large portion of their days within their ambit. As is the case in books for adults, in children's stories teachers are represented in diverse ways: as fair, competent, and even-handed or as snide and cruel.

Often teachers fulfil a precise role within the narrative. In many stories they patrol an equilibrium, a norm, that is disrupted as the events of the story unfold. At the end of the tale order is re-established when the conflict is resolved. So stories are structured round conflict: the status quo is challenged, and its defenders and opponents clash, leading to change, to resolution of the conflict and perhaps to the protagonists and antagonists gaining insight into their situation. Teachers are therefore associated with that safe, often boring, predictable base from which characters move out and away, towards self-awareness and growth. School is useful from a narrative point of view, because, like the Rovers' Return in *Coronation Street*, it allows the writers to assemble disparate characters who might otherwise not want to have anything to do with each other. In such places conflict can credibly simmer, and chance meetings can occur naturally. One example of this is found in Frank Murphy's story, *Dark Secret* (2000), in which David comes to live with his grandfather after his mother dies and his father takes to the drink. The locals taunt him with the insult 'killer's breed', and school provides the location in which he can display his strength and his values in a showdown with fellow pupil, Ruction, the enemy who becomes his friend. But the teachers in this school establish standards of justice that contrast with those in the community outside. The principal teacher is nicknamed Agatha Christie because of her ability to get to the bottom of mysteries, and the science teacher, Dracula, is at hand to guide and support with a light touch. Matthew Sweeney's *A Man, a Boy and a ... Fox* (2002) also has a wise, enabling, if rather under-developed (from the narrative point of view) head teacher. Martina Murphy's award-winning *Dirt Tracks* (2000) is another example of a teacher who fulfils a crucial role in the plot. The story's narrator, Nick, is awkward, inattentive, bashful and short on self-esteem. He is slow to concede that a teacher could believe in him and refuses to accept her positive appraisal of his writing until he wins a coveted award. However, it is noteworthy that this is a story without a happy ending, and the point driven home is that the support of a teacher is not enough to hold back the tide of domestic and social troubles.

The competition that is unavoidable in school and the resentment against authority that is predictable among the young mean that characters can create alliances against teachers, who are (as we have already seen) the first line of defence of authority and authoritarianism in society. So many children's stories relate to the problems created or exacerbated by teachers who are blind to the complexities of their students' lives. The teacher then embodies what the pupils have to fight against, what they have to survive. One example of this may be found in Gillian Perdue's *Adam's Starling* (2001), in which Adam, the victim of the school's bullies, is blamed by a teacher for fighting with a boy smaller than himself when in fact he has been tripped by the bullies. In a pattern that is repeated over and over again in the portrayal of teachers, this teacher – and significantly in this story, she is the unnamed 'teacher on duty' – snaps commands and imposes punishments, deaf to Adam's entreaties. Here we see parallels: the schoolyard bullies' behaviour is replicated by the teacher, who might be expected to be the arbiter of justice. The bullies abuse their superior size and exercise power without authority; she draws on her legitimate authority, but does not allow it to constrain or inform her comment. However, while the teacher is wrong in this instance, in that she refuses to listen, the authority of her profession is not lessened. Miss Hill, the class teacher, is a model of fairness, and the principal teacher Mrs Malley dispenses justice like Solomon. One might deduce that if these teachers are the representatives of society's figures of authority, then one need have no serious fears. Individuals may act hastily, but the higher the position people occupy in the hierarchy of power, the more trustworthy they are.

In some stories, teachers are depicted on a continuum from bumbling, ineffectual idiots to willing but inferior helpers or facilitators of students who themselves by contrast are efficient, intelligent and, to varying degrees, sensible. At one end of the trajectory is Creina Mansfield's *It Wasn't Me* (2001), in which the headmaster and the other teachers are breezy, competent, but quite detached from the lives of their pupils. Teacher incompetence as the butt of humour is commonly the case in school stories from the earlier part of the twentieth century in particular. This is exemplified by a series begun in *Our Boys* in 1922 entitled 'The Fourth Classical', a fantastical story about secret codes, wild adventures and escapes. The mystery of the location of the Black and Tans' arms is finally resolved, not by the masters of the school, St Finbar's, but by the intrepid pupils, with some assistance from their teacher, Mr McGrath. Here we see the Christian Brothers borrowing the form from the English school story which has been immensely popular since the 1880s and continued to be successful into the 1960s in the hands of writers such as Anthony Buckeridge, creator of the Jennings series. The tradition, slightly updated, continues. Stephanie Dagg has written a tale for younger readers, *Oh Teacher!* (2001), in which a well-meaning but ineffectual and rather silly teacher allows priceless museum artefacts to be smashed, before being lost in a maze, from which she is rescued by a police helicopter. Even worse, the story ends with her having learned nothing from the experience, and about to repeat the pandemonium. A variation on such a teacher may be found in Martina Murphy's award-winning *Dirt Tracks*, a religion teacher who is living with an ex-pupil and uses her class to talk about everything from Brussels sprouts to contraception.

Clichés of nastiness abound in contemporary stories in which schools figure. One story that combines that stereotype with the notion of the teacher as the physician who needs to heal himself may be found in David Donohue's *Walter Speazlebug* (2002). Mr Strong constantly shoots a volley of imperatives at his pupils, and sadistically criticises Walter's beloved grandfather, an ill, old man. Walter enables Mr Strong to see that he should have followed his desire to be a carpenter, and to leave behind the role of teacher to which he is clearly not suited. He flings off the tablecloth that covers the stool beside Mr Strong's desk to reveal beautiful, intricate carving. Significantly, Mr Strong opens his mouth to scream but nothing comes out. He is the one who has been silenced, while Walter, the dreamer, interprets the incident with a wisdom and insight beyond his years: 'You're not a teacher, Mr Strong, and you know it. You were never meant to be a teacher – it was not your gift.' The story ends with Mr Strong, having listened to Walter, on his way to London to start a new life.

A variation of this theme may be found in Malachy Doyle's *Who is Jessie Flood?* (2002). Jessie is an alienated fourteen-year-old unfortunate to be caught in the grip of a teacher nicknamed Frostbite. Vitriol belches forth from him in an endless stream. After a particularly vicious and self-pitying outburst from the teacher, Jessie responds with an impassioned defence of the value of the truth, of youngsters needing to think for themselves. The outraged Frostbite retaliates by condemning Jessie's insolence and lack of respect, and by ejecting him from the classroom over which he has dominion. But Jessie's words reverberate with a deep wisdom: the child is father to the man, and the narrator of the story clearly sympathises with Jessie's values, whereas the teacher's are reminiscent of Maura Laverty's teacher-character and belong to another age.

Tony Hickey's short-story 'Saying Goodbye' from Gordon Snell's collection, *Thicker than Water* (2001), is about the last day at secondary school. The story manipulates its audience into siding with the teachers and perceiving not righteous indignation, but the adolescent impatience of the pupils. 'Conor was lucky that his teachers, whom he described as "a bunch of creeps", were so patient with him. All they did was keep him back after school or make him stand in the corridor until Mr Murphy [the principal teacher] encountered him on one of his rounds of inspection and verbally wiped the floor with him.' Yet a few pages on we learn that the boys are scared that if, for even the most innocent reason, they catch the eye of one of the teachers, they may become the target of his anger. We learn that the central character, Conor, has a strained relationship with his father, comparable to that between Gar and his shopkeeper father in *Philadelphia, Here I Come!* and his anger is transferred onto those other symbols of authority, the teachers.

The ambivalent relationship between teachers and children has several variations. In Michael Morpurgo's *The Ghost of Grania O'Malley* (1996), the teacher offers a reactionary and unreconstructed version of the myth-history of Grania O'Malley, who she descibes as a scarlet woman. Her blindness to facts is also evident in her throwaway cruelty to Jessie, who suffers from what she calls 'cerebral bloody palsy': Jessie could try harder, she proclaims. Given a hundred lines to write because she told the truth – and not the lie that the teacher believes it to be – her mother tacitly accepts the teacher's authority, even though they see through the teacher, and they embarrass Jessie by replaying a video that dwells on her disability rather than her strength and achievement. The story ends with the teacher accepting the error of her ways. Significantly, she takes no part in the community effort to save the island from the claws of the developers.

Perhaps the children's book in which the most complex relationship exists between teacher and pupil is in Mark O'Sullivan's *White Lies* (1997). Tom, the adoptive parent of the teenage protagonist Nance is also a teacher, and so the boundaries between the public and private roles are blurred. As Nance becomes more estranged from her parents because she believes they lied to her about her natural parents, Tom, the exemplary teacher – wise, concerned, involved-but-from-a-critical-distance – is unable to learn his own lessons. More than other teacher-portraits, his comes to embody the familiar contemporary authority figure whose jurisdiction is questioned, and the Ireland he inhabits would be utterly foreign to the great bulk of the stories already cited. In it disaffected teenagers – some gay, some drunken – grapple with a deep sense of hopelessness. Certainties also evade their teacher who knows he ought not unduly pressurise his rather manipulative, misguided daughter and, as the crisis deepens, his confidence in his authority evaporates. It transpires that Nance's natural father was a black African teacher, a good man made bad by drugs, who was killed in a car crash after a showdown with Tom, her mother's new boyfriend. What is exceptional about this story is that the teachers depicted are complex characters whose lives go often awry, and their authority and status are no guarantors of certainty. This is also a point at which Nance arrives at a moment of self-realisation, when she recognises that there is an alternative way of looking at the world, a perspective beyond her own. Such episodes mark the moment when the process of being absorbed into public society takes hold. Nance begins to see her individual cares and battles as related to more abstract concepts such as fairness and honour, and the need to strive against adversity.

Why is it, then, that negative images of teachers predominate in Irish literature, given that most of us treasure memories of teachers who, as W. B. Yeats put it, lit a fire rather than filled a pail? For one thing, evil and negativity are more interesting and more diverse in their forms than good. Teachers' evil deeds attract attention for their variety – evil is a necessary ingredient of the conflict that creates a good yarn. Furthermore, the tendency to perceive Irish subjects of the British empire as mere children was replicated by Irish nationalist leaders in the nineteenth and twentieth century who were themselves prone to perceive and address their supporters as children. So a tension already underlies the relationship between children and their teachers.

Despite the suspicion they seem to engender in adult writers as much as in their pupils, teachers occupy a central role in transmitting the values of society. Much is asked of them. They are expected to provide cultural and moral leadership and, in an ideal world, to personify and distil what a society considers best and most worthy of preservation. Theirs are the voices of legitimacy, and the writer tacitly positions the reader either to accept and endorse them, or to interrogate and reject them. Perhaps it is not so much the teachers as individuals but the values that they disseminate and represent that are, so often and so consistently, challenged.

CHAPTER TEN

The Schoolmaster in the New State

John Coolahan

There are few personal memoirs or studies of the role, position and experience of the primary teacher in the early decades of the independent Irish state. This is surprising for a number of reasons including that from the time of 'the teachers' rebellion', as the 1916 rising has often been called, teachers took a significant role in the independence movement. It is also surprising in that teachers tended to play a very central and intimate role in community life during these decades. In setting out an article on this theme with a particular focus on the work of Bryan MacMahon, who did leave us with the valuable memoir, *The Master*, a number of questions arise which are worthy of exploration. These include the following:

What was the cultural background?
What was the educational context?
What were the educational priorities in 1922?
How was curricular policy developed?
What was the traditional image of the teacher?
How was teacher training conducted?
What was the school management system?
What was the style of school inspection?

What was the role of the primary certificate?

What were teachers' salaries and conditions of work?

What was the condition of school buildings?

What drove vocational and professional commitment?

Answers to such questions may lead us to understand the policy context, the professional environment and the day-to-day realities of teachers in the half century following independence, the period in which Bryan MacMahon gave distinguished service as a teacher. Some of the answers also highlight the difficult and challenging environment it was for teachers, and suggest a subtitle to the article: 'Vocational Commitment in the Face of Adversity'.

The Cultural and Educational Background

The roots of the cultural climate which prevailed in the post-independence period lie in the revival of cultural nationalism which began during the last decades of the nineteenth century. This involved the re-discovery and evaluation of the Gaelic heritage. A remarkable revival of interest took place in the Irish language, literature, history and myth, music, folksong and dance, games and artistic achievements. Among key manifestations of this enthusiasm was the establishment of new organisations to promote public interest in this cultural heritage such as the Gaelic Athletic Association (1884), the National Literary Society (1892), and the Gaelic League (1893). The league established its own newspaper, *An Claidheamh Solais* and undertook a multiplicity of activities promoting Irish cultural activities, becoming one of the most remarkable adult education agencies of its time. By 1904, it had 600 branches and was organising Irish language classes, *feiseanna* and *aeraíochtaí* throughout the country, with, from 1897, its great national cultural festival, an tOireachtas, on an annual basis. Other newspapers came on the scene such as *The United Irishman* (1898) and *The Leader* (1900) which emphasised the cultural distinctiveness of the Irish heritage. The founding of the Abbey Theatre as a national theatre in 1904 while being 'a cradle of genius' also gave rise to controversy in its dramatic representations of Irish life and character. Striking personalities of the day such as Douglas Hyde, Eoin MacNeill, W. B. Yeats, Pearse and O'Growney provided charismatic leadership in promoting the cultural nationalist cause.

Among key tenets of the ideology of cultural nationalism was an emphasis on the possession of a distinct language as the most vital component of nationhood. It was held that a people expresses itself best through its ancestral language which has been shaped as an appropriate vehicle to represent the psyche of a people. It also stressed the centrality of the school as an agency of national regeneration. It was held that the school had been used as a major tool by imperialist forces to suppress or marginalise traditional Irish language and culture. The trend should be reversed in the cause of the revival of that culture. Inherent in the cultural nationalist belief was that a nation which could demonstrate that it possessed a distinct language had a right to achieve statehood to protect its nationality. It was within this latter tenet that a blending of cultural and political nationalism took place in the move towards independence.

Cultural nationalism was, thus, a major current of thought in the lead-up to independence. There was also another strong movement, that of administrative reform. In the spring of 1919 two reports were presented to the British parliament for the reform of Irish education. The Killanin Report set out proposed reforms for primary education, and the Molony Report made recommendations for the radical reform of secondary education. On the basis of these reports an education bill was prepared and got its first reading in parliament in December 1919. This was the most radical and comprehensive effort at the reform of Irish education ever proposed. However, it ran into prolonged controversy, and the strong opposition of the Catholic Church, which saw in its administrative proposals a diminution in the control of schooling which it had won for itself in the nineteenth century. Public opinion became polarised in the intense debate, with the teachers strongly in favour of the bill, which among other things promised them increased salaries and improved conditions of work. Eventually, in December 1920, the Education Bill was withdrawn, just a week before the Government of Ireland Act establishing partition was enacted.[1] This was the last attempt at educational legislation for the whole island; henceforth very different policies would prevail for education within the two administrations, north and south. The controversy on the withdrawn Education Bill cast a long shadow on subsequent developments. One outcome was the awareness of politicians that interference with Church influence on education was a hazardous undertaking. So, as well as the travail of the War of Independence and the Civil War, the new state inherited an education system badly in need of reform, but about which there had been recent and bitter controversy.

The Educational Policy Priorities of the New State

With the establishment in difficult circumstances of the new state, the educational policy priorities were very much in the ambit of the cultural nationalist movement, rather than in administrative reform. It was interesting that the first Dáil in 1919 had established a 'ministry for Irish', rather than a 'ministry for education'. However, on the transition to independence in 1922, the Irish Free State appointed a minister for education and, in 1924, set up the Department of Education under the Ministries and Secretaries Act. The other administrative initiatives taken were the School Attendance Act of 1926, the establishment of preparatory colleges in 1926 and the Vocational Education Act of 1930. The most striking feature of the transition to native education rule was continuity, rather than radical administrative change.

The priority of educational policy was for curricular change. This was trenchantly articulated by the new chief officer of the minister, Pádraig Ó Brolcháin, when he addressed a meeting of the Commissioners of National Education on 31 January 1922. He told them:

> In the administration of Irish education it is the intention of the new Government to work with all its might for the strengthening of the national fibre by giving the language, history, music and tradition of Ireland their natural place in the life of Irish schools.[2]

It was also made clear to them that they were not viewed as part of the process of implementation, and so, after ninety years of existence, the board of commissioners was dissolved.

Even before the formal establishment of independence, on the initiative of the Irish National Teachers' Organisation (INTO), in 1920, a national programme conference had been convened to frame a primary school programme to 'suit Irish needs and conditions'. Its report was issued in January 1922, and was immediately adopted as national policy by the new minister, Micheál Ó h-Aodha. The two key features of this programme were the reduction of the range of subjects in the child-centred programme which had been in existence since 1900, and the giving of a central place on the programme to the Irish language. Accordingly, subjects such as drawing and elementary science were dropped and Irish became a compulsory subject for one hour a day in all schools. Irish became the sole language of the infant school. Most subjects were to be taught through the medium of Irish. Irish history, music and traditions were to get more attention.[3] This involved a significant challenge to teachers as at that time only nine per cent of primary teachers had 'bilingual certificates' and were deemed competent to teach through the medium of Irish. A further twenty-three per cent held 'ordinary certificates', but these were not regarded as sufficient indicators of proficiency in the language to teach through its medium.

It was not surprising then that the INTO, at its annual congress in 1925, pressed for a second programme conference to re-evaluate the situation. This second programme conference was convened by the Minister for Education, Eoin MacNeill, and reported in 1926. While endorsing the approach taken in the 1922 programme, it recommended a more transitional, gradual approach. In line with this, higher and lower courses were designed for Irish and English, with the higher course taken in the predominant language of the school. A modification was also made on the all-Irish infant school programme to help teachers achieve the objectives for Irish: a lightening of the programme for mathematics, history and geography was introduced. Thus, a somewhat modified programme was put in place from 1926.[4]

The third stage in the evolution of the primary curriculum

took place in 1934, following the accession to power of the Fianna Fáil party in 1932. It had criticised the allegedly slow progress of the schools in the language revival campaign. The Minister for Education, Thomas Derrig, stated in the Dáil:

> I have always had in mind the fact that the effort to revive Irish as a spoken language undoubtedly rests very largely with our schools. The responsibility rests with the schools to do that work. It is through their instrumentality that we hope to achieve success.[5]

The revised programme issued by the minister in 1934 lightened the existing programme further by dropping rural science, reducing further the programme in mathematics and a 'less ambitious programme in English'. The all-Irish infant school was restored and extended to include first class. All schools now took the higher course in Irish and the lower course in English.[6] Thus, it is clear that a determined bid was to be made to ensure that as far as the school programme could foster it, Irish was to be the predominant subject in the primary school education of Irish children. The primary school curriculum devised by 1934 was to remain the curricular policy up to 1971, with a modification of the infant school programme in 1948. The effort by the teachers to broaden the policy approach as represented by the INTO's Plan for Education, in 1947, was not successful. Thus, the curriculum which Bryan MacMahon and his contemporaries were required to implement was a narrow 3-R type programme, with two languages, Irish being the one most favoured.

The Traditional Image of the Teacher
One of the striking features of Irish educational history is the depth and rootedness of regard for the teacher. Even in the most difficult political, economic and social circumstances in

the past there is evidence of the respect for learning and those who had it, such as teachers, among the common people. For instance, it is a striking fact that before any state support and, at times, in the face of state opposition, as in the penal law era, Irish people went to considerable lengths to get schooling for their children. The educational census of 1824 records that as many as 9,330 hedge schools were in operation. These were very much 'schools of the people, for the people and by the people'. The hedge schoolmaster was well regarded and esteemed by local communities who sought out his services and who sustained him. Bryan MacMahon was very conscious of that old tradition and remarks in *The Master*, 'The love of learning had been passed on in the locality by the old hedge-school masters, Dinny Dillane and the Bachall Stack'. When the national school system was established in 1831, the commissioners issued rules and regulations. Their conception of the teacher was of one who led by leadership and example in the extolled work of young people's formation. Regrettably, however, this role was not reciprocated in the remuneration of the teachers, which was always minimal and parsimonious. Yet, despite the lack of adequate remuneration the high social regard was sustained. Following political independence these two aspects of the situation continued. Teachers continued to be poorly paid, but the communities within which they worked tended to regard them with respect, and valued their work. Apart from their work in the schools, many of the teachers also contributed much to local community life and social activities, which also won them regard. Teachers such as Bryan MacMahon were inheritors of this tradition and, in their turn, did much to sustain it, and contribute to it.

The Training of Teachers in the New State

As MacMahon relates in *The Master*, it was his mother who persuaded him to enter for the King's Scholarship, by which the examination for entry to the teacher training college was known at that time. He was successful and entered St Patrick's Training College, Drumcondra. Its way of academic and social life was reflective of the other training colleges, as they continued a nineteenth-century model of the formation and socialisation of the national teaching force. Both State and Church took great care that the students be moulded in the desired shape. The colleges were boarding in the full sense, with only limited time approved for social life outside the colleges. The colleges were all single sex. They were denominationally run and religious services were observed at early morning, late evening and on all religious festivals. The daily timetables were very full, with heavy lecture loads and allocated times for all functions.

The academic life of the colleges was very much under Department of Education control, whose staff set the examinations, corrected students' scripts and conducted practical teaching tests. From the early 1920s Irish became a compulsory subject for entry to the colleges. It was also to be the medium of instruction and the official language of the colleges for social communication. To improve the supply of Irish-speaking students, the preparatory colleges were established by the state in 1926, and were to be administered by denominational groups. During the 1920s practising teachers were provided with a range of in-service courses in Irish.

In 1931, the form of recruitment to the colleges was changed. It was now to be based on the results of students in the leaving certificate examination, coupled with oral examinations in

Irish, English and music, known as the 'Easter Orals'. In 1932–33 the courses in the colleges were re-structured, with more attention being paid to studies in education. An ongoing problem was the availability of textbooks on education in the Irish language. However, great reliance was placed on lecture notes given in Irish and not much emphasis was placed on library study or personal reflection by students. The timetable and other demands on students tended to keep them very occupied, as attendance at lectures and functions was compulsory.[7] Interestingly, the young MacMahon's personal qualities must have appealed to the college authorities, as he was appointed senior prefect, a prestigious, if demanding, role among the student body. MacMahon was probably not unusual in the lack of pleasure he records from his student days, about 1929–30, when he records: 'Studying and the onerous duties as senior prefect made my stay a doleful one that, at times, threatened to undermine my health.'[8]

'The Powers That Be' … School Managers

The school manager, in the person of the local parish priest or Protestant clergyman, was a formidable figure with multi-faceted powers in the primary school system. These had been hard fought for during the century prior to independence. On the eve of independence, the Catholic clerical managers of national schools issued a statement which clearly indicated their intentions to retain the powers which had been won:

> In view of pending changes in Irish education, we wish to assert the great fundamental principle that the only satisfactory system of education for Catholics is one wherein Catholic children are taught in Catholic schools by Catholic teachers under Catholic control.[9]

The newly independent state was careful not to disturb in any way the powers of the national school managers. Among the key powers were those of appointment and dismissal. The power of appointment was frequently exercised in an arbitrary manner, and was often linked to local family status or connections. In the opening pages of *The Master*, MacMahon gives a humorous account of how the local school manager responded to the entreaties of MacMahon's mother, who was herself a teacher in the parish:

> 'Here he is, canon,' she said. 'I hope you won't refuse him the appointment.' The ferret dangling from my hand, I turned. Appointment! I wanted no appointment. I already had a teaching job in Dublin and was happy enough with it. The old canon turned his head, 'I'll give you the position,' he wheezed. I was flabbergasted.[10]

MacMahon had already secured a job in Donore Avenue in Dublin and wished to stay there. However, he now was awarded a job in Listowel and was prevailed upon to accept it. Such bizarre styles of appointment recur in much teacher lore in the period, a notable other instance being in Jack Brosnahan's memoirs on his visit to the manager of a school near Knocknagoshel about the same time in the early 1930s.

Managers had the power to supervise the general work of the schools and, in a particular way, the religious instruction in the schools. The teacher's preparation of pupils for first communion, confirmation and the annual religious examinations came under particular scrutiny. The formal *quid pro quo* for the managerial role was the maintenance of the local school from parish funds, with small capitation grants from the state. However, this responsibility was honoured more in the breach than in the observance. The condition of many national schools, most inherited from the nineteenth century, was lamentable and the state tended to see school maintenance as a local responsibility. Some managers took an enlightened interest, others were neglectful of this responsibility. For much of the period involving 'the hungry thirties', followed by the privations of war-time and the economic recession of the 1950s, financial resources for school improvement were not easily come by. However, it is also the case that culpable neglect was often in evidence. It was this which prompted the INTO in the early 1950s to campaign for reform in local school management by seeking to make school maintenance a charge on the public purse. This was deeply resented by the Catholic hierarchy who wanted no interference whatever with school management, even if school managers were unable to fulfil their obligations of school maintenance. In the climate of the time, it was not too surprising that the INTO desisted from its campaign following a strong statement on the issue by the Catholic primate, Cardinal d'Alton, in 1954. The issue was not resolved, however, and the unsatisfactory nature of school buildings continued to be a feature of primary schooling. Eventually, following an INTO strike focused on Ardfert School in north Kerry in 1967–68, school managers adopted a more enlightened approach in the context of a modernising Ireland. Byran Mac-Mahon bears eloquent witness to the appalling condition of school buildings at the time and how they impinged on the educational life of the school – this is dealt with in a later section of this chapter.

'The Powers that Be' ... Inspectors
There had long been a tradition of difficult relationships between the inspectorate and teachers. The Dill Commission of

1913 supported the objections of teachers to inspectorial practice. It recommended reforms, but most of these did not come to pass. Following independence, newly appointed inspectors saw themselves in the vanguard of the language revival movement through the schools. The INTO pressed for, and got, a committee to review the inspectorate and it reported in 1927. It found that the disciplinary, controlling function of the inspectorate was uppermost, rather than the pedagogical advisory one. It recommended improvements in the work practices of the inspectorate and recommended that an appeal procedure be put in place for teachers who had a grievance on their treatment. Despite this, difficulties continued. The grading of teachers by inspectors into 'Highly Efficient', 'Efficient' and 'Inefficient' became linked to the teacher's achievements in raising the standard of Irish among pupils, without taking into account the socio-economic and geographical context of the school.[11]

In 1929, also, the primary certificate examination was introduced as a voluntary examination to be taken by pupils at the end of sixth class in primary school. Teachers objected to this form of pupil evaluation. However, their views were not taken up and in 1943 the primary certificate examination in Irish, English and arithmetic became a compulsory examination for all sixth class primary pupils. An Taoiseach, Éamon de Valera, was a force behind this decision and stated in the Dáil:

> I do not care what teachers are offended by it. I am less interested in the teacher's method of teaching than I am in the results he achieves, and the test I would apply would be the test of an examination.[12]

He also favoured the grading system for teachers and opposed the abolition of the 'Highly Efficient' grade in 1949, holding that rewards and punishments were what motivated people. The primary certificate was not abolished until 1967, at the instigation of the INTO, which held that it had a counter-educational effect.

Bryan MacMahon has left some revealing perspectives on the inspectorate as he encountered it as a schoolmaster in the new state. His judgement was:

> The inspection system was over-rigorous. No idealistic goal can be achieved by fear: it must be inspired by a kind of dynamic of contagious love. The inspectorate contained many brilliant and understanding men, but there were among them those of parochial outlook who did not understand the profound nature of what was at stake; since they did not possess a vision, they were unable to impart one to others. The department to which they were answerable continued, more or less, to impose a system of examination with the attitudes of overlordship that had obtained in colonial days. Motivation was but dimly understood.[13]

MacMahon also gives us a vibrant pen picture of his encounter with an over-weening divisional inspector examining a group of nine year olds on the intricacies of Irish grammar on a miserably wet, cold day. Having observed this process MacMahon relates as follows:

> By now I had more than enough. Here were the sick remnants of one of the best classes I had ever taught. In it were children who could gabble in Irish, as the saying goes, 'till the cows came home'. And here was an inspector who wanted to find out not what the children knew but what they did not know. Was it me he wished to impress?
>
> For one of the very few occasions in my teaching life, I decided to revolt. I called the inspector aside quietly and said under

my breath, 'Look at the sick children in this wretched school, most of whom should be in bed this appalling day. Look at the meagre fire around which they are huddled. And you come in to confuse them with esoteric cases of nouns and tenses of verbs. Let me tell you, sir, that if you and the likes of you are not checked you will give our beautiful language a grammarian's funeral.'

He looked at me in astonishment. I don't think any pedagogic dog had ever barked back at him before. He walked quietly out the door.[14]

Because of the power of the inspector, it was not easy for teachers to stand up against instances of authoritarian behaviour when it occurred on the part of inspectors at the time. In this instance, no dire consequences were visited on MacMahon, who records that on a later visit the inspector engaged in a more collegial manner.

Teacher Salaries in the New State

One of the great breakthroughs ever on primary teacher salaries occurred on the eve of independence. Realising that the Education Bill of 1919–20 was running into major difficulties, the INTO, in the autumn of 1920, succeeded in instigating separate negotiations on the promised new salary deal. In November 1920, a week before a wages standstill order was imposed, a landmark salary package was achieved. It introduced a salary scale for men of £170 over twenty-three years to reach a maximum of £415. For women the starting point was £155 and it reached a maximum of £330. There were also extra allowances for qualifications and responsibility. Teachers were very pleased at the improved salary scales these figures involved. However, they were not to enjoy them for long, and it was to be a long time before they re-attained these salary levels.

For teachers who envisaged the achievement of independence as heralding better times for them, they were in for a rude awakening. Following the Great War there was a decline in the cost of living. The new Irish government was faced with many difficulties, including financial constraints. It looked to make savings from the public service and primary teachers were the category which suffered most. In 1923 they experienced a salary cut of ten per cent. This was followed in 1934 by a further salary cut of nine per cent, though this blow was somewhat softened by the introduction of a non-contributory pension scheme for primary teachers. With no salary increase, but rather deductions of nineteen per cent in their salaries, teachers were poorly positioned for the 'hungry thirties'.

Many teachers in the 1930s were unemployed, and new training college graduates found it difficult to obtain permanent positions. In 1934 the 'marriage ban' was introduced, whereby henceforth women entering the profession would have to resign if they married. A few years later the retirement age for women was reduced from sixty-five to sixty years which was opposed by women teachers for a number of reasons including the difficulty this imposed of building up forty consecutive years of service for pension purposes. In 1936 new limits were placed on the numbers being admitted to teacher training colleges, and in the early 1940s some colleges even closed for a period.

After sixteen years of independence the teachers got a salary award of five per cent in 1938, which in no way brought them to the salary levels they enjoyed from 1920 to 1923. In 1939 the Second World War broke out, which was to last for six years. Ireland established a neutrality stance but, of course, did not escape war-time privations with shortages of commodities responded to by the introduction of ration cards. The cost of living increased significantly, but a wages standstill order was imposed. The only possibility of redress was through wartime bonuses. But, again, national teachers did worse than other categories of the public service. In January 1943 they eventually got a small war-time bonus which did very little to alleviate the hardship and difficulties being encountered. Teacher patience was growing very thin. In December 1944 the INTO lodged a salary claim on the following terms:

Married Men		Single Men and Women	
Min	Max	Min	Max
£350	£650	£300	£600

Protracted negotiations followed and, eventually, in December 1945, the government made the following salary offer:[15]

Married Men		Single Men		Women	
Min	Max	Min	Max	Min	Max
£220	£485	£220	£380	£200	£340

The gap between claim and offer was very wide indeed. With no improvement on offer from the government the INTO took the rare step of declaring a strike. The strike strategy involved teachers in Dublin withdrawing their services and teachers throughout the country contributing a salary levy in their support. As time went on, the strike became a major issue of public debate. Despite pressures on it from a variety of sources, including members of the Catholic hierarchy, the government refused to budge from its position. The bitter dispute lasted for seven months, until October 1946. By this time, serious problems were being encountered in Dublin and, at the request of Archbishop John Charles McQuaid, the INTO agreed to call off its strike. The INTO lost the battle but, perhaps, not the war. Interestingly, the strike experience strengthened the INTO and emphasised the need for union solidarity in the face of what was seen as an intransigent government. The strike became an important part of INTO folklore and under new leadership from 1947 the union became a much stronger force. The INTO published its radical Plan for Education in 1947 which sought fundamental changes in the primary curriculum, but official policy remained unaltered until the 1971 curriculum was introduced. Many teachers became disenchanted with Fianna Fáil and were instrumental in securing a change of government in the 1948 general election, ending sixteen successive years of Fianna Fáil government.

The new coalition government (1948–51) was more accommodating to teachers' needs. Following the Roe Commission of 1949 improvements in salary took place, in 1950 a Council of Education was established and, in 1951, teachers obtained a Conciliation and Arbitration scheme for salary negotiations. The next major salary battle of the INTO was securing salary parity with secondary and vocational teachers. This was only won following difficult battles in the wake of the Ryan Tribunal of 1968. By 1972 all teachers enjoyed a common salary scale, with extra allowances for qualifications and the exercise of responsibility, and a common Conciliation and Arbitration scheme was agreed for all. In 1973 equal salaries for men and women teachers were achieved.

Throughout his teaching career from 1931 to the early 1970s Bryan MacMahon was one of those teachers in the early decades of the new state who experienced much privation in terms of remuneration. Many teachers had to supplement their earnings by other activities. MacMahon himself records, 'To augment my miserly salary just before the Second World War I opened a bookshop in my wife's name in the main street, where my house was'.[16] By the year of his retirement he had seen major improvements achieved, and the beginning of a process which was to buttress the teachers' position in society.

School Buildings and Conditions of Work

Independent Ireland inherited a very extensive infrastructure of national schools, but many of them were old, small and in bad condition. Apart from some school amalgamations in the 1920s, the government never adopted a strategic policy to improve the overall quality of the national school buildings. The quality of provision was very uneven with some schools well maintained and equipped, while many others were unsatisfactory locations for the important role of educating the young generations. For the vast majority of Irish children national schooling was the only formal education they got. It is a credit to Bryan MacMahon that he has left us frank accounts of the school circumstances in which he worked in the town of Listowel which can stand as representative of the conditions faced by many national teachers.

MacMahon had been a pupil at the school, which dated from 1836, in which he was from 1931 to be employed as a teacher. This is his graphic account of the physical environment in which he was now expected to teach:

Now, as a teacher, I viewed it with hostile eyes. A large pool of stagnant water reposed at the side of the gate as one entered. When an inspector commented adversely on the pool I turned back the pages of an old report book and showed that the same pool had been adversely commented on in the 1870s.

Water from this pool seeped under the building, rendering it perpetually damp. Beyond this pool was a toilet of sorts with a great water tank overhead. The three open cubicles were in a perpetual state of dampness and enormously soiled. There was one toilet equipped with a door for all the teachers, male and female. The building itself was grim; four windows upstairs and four downstairs were set in naked limestone facing north.

There was one tap for some 350 children. The handle of the tap had long since snapped off, so that the water seemed either perpetually running or perpetually cut off. Strong pliers could sometimes get movement – off or on – from the tap. Nine times out of ten the water overflowed the metal trough and poured down into the hallway. Thence it seeped into the locked-up area beneath the stairwell, where a single rail of turf was stored for the miserable school fires.

Heating and cleaning in the school were almost non-existent. The cleaning was done by poorer boys kept in after school ...

The fireplaces were holes in the wall into which damp turf was dumped. It took an hour or more before the fire reddened, but little or no heat came forth: there really was smoke without fire. In the interests of safety, fireguards were introduced at some stage. On a wet day the fireguards were festooned with steaming sodden clothes. The desks were long and had holes containing pottery inkwells. The ink we made ourselves out of ink powder; for obvious reasons the inkwells were a source of constant amusement to the children.

The twenty pounds allocated to each school per year for heating and cleaning was grossly inadequate. We had no caretaker, little running water, less light, no heat – just one squalid mess.[17]

MacMahon goes on to refer to the unwelcome rodent inhabitants found in many old school buildings – 'The rats in the old school building were brazen. Their noses could be seen twitching at lunchtime. During the Christmas holiday the bottoms of the doors were gnawed away as a consequence of rodent famine'.[18] Despite the continued existence of some sub-standard schools today, it may be difficult for contemporaries to accept this dismal portrayal of how things were, but many teachers and pupils of that era would have no difficulty in recalling such school conditions.

Like many teachers, MacMahon fought long and hard to get improvements. Letters were sent to the school manager outlining the difficulties and emphasising the health hazard of the filthy toilets. He records 'The result was a silence as of the tomb'. Undeterred, he and his colleague Frank Sheehy adopted more sophisticated tactics which eventually roused the concordance of the bishop and the county medical officer. The teachers got a photographer to take pictures of children in the unsavoury school conditions, and held these in reserve. Mac-Mahon clearly states that he saw his school as a test case standing 'for many hundreds of substandard – to use a mild word – schools in Ireland in which hundreds or even thousands of teachers were forced to teach and which children had to attend. This, thirty or more years after the foundation of our adventurous new state!'

Eventually, a meeting on the school issue was arranged with the Minister for Education, Dick Mulcahy, a veteran of the War of Independence. As the meeting did not seem to be achieving much, MacMahon chose his moment to intervene, as he states:

I watched my opportunity carefully. When the sheaf of photographs was being examined, with the Minister equably asking, 'What have we here?' I, until then a back-room boy, broke in in

Irish, saying, 'I will explain, Minister.' Walking forward to the table, I said, 'You see these mud-spattered children?' 'Yes,' he said. 'The first boy there is a grandnephew of Michael Collins. The second boy covered in mud in the school yard is the grandson of a man who sat in the first Dáil with you and was a member of your party. Thirdly, this boy clothed in muck from head to foot is a nephew of Thomas Ashe, who, as history records, fought with you in north Dublin in the Easter Rising, a man who subsequently died as a result of forced feeding while on hunger-strike. You will bear with me, Minister, if I say that these, the inheritors of your revolution, were rewarded with squalor.'[19]

This vignette of focused opportunism made its point, and a new school was authorised by Mulcahy's successor, Seán Moylan, also a veteran of the War of Independence. MacMahon captures well the impact of the new building for teachers, pupils and parents:

From the day our new school was built a dynamic era began for the children of our locality. The paint-bright rooms almost blinded us with their marvellous colours; I have nothing but praise for the architect and contractor. The new manager ensured that the staff were consulted at every phase of the work. It was a lovely building, with a Séamus Murphy statue above the main doorway. The teachers and I persuaded the parents to knit multi-coloured geansaís for the children. When the inspector arrived he blinked at the riot of colour before him ... It was a joy to work in the new building.[20]

MacMahon's Approach to Teaching
It would not be possible to do full justice to MacMahon's approach to teaching in a short space. However, in reflecting on the theme of the schoolmaster in the new state, while the insights on teaching emerge from MacMahon's personal con-

sciousness some are also representative of the values of other teachers of his generation, and should be touched upon in such a reflection.

In the first instance, we note MacMahon locating himself in his cultural hinterland, 'In the townlands stretching north and west to the Shannon and south to Tralee there was a fine tradition of scholarship. The holdings were small and the families large, and the traditional escape was by education. North Kerry boasted of three university presidents at that time: O'Rahilly of Cork, Coffey of Dublin, and Kissane of Maynooth … Thus, I would count on a tradition that implied that education was not a foreign body set down among the pupils but something that their forbears had respect for.'[21] MacMahon was also acutely aware of the richness of the heritage of folklore, dialect, song and story of the locale and set out to harvest it. We also get a sense of the fresh young schoolmaster taking his bearings:

> First of all, I was resolved to praise, for 'Mol an óige agus tiocfaidh sí; cáin an óige and críonfaidh sí' – praise youth and it will come; disparage youth and it will wither. An instrument of education, that's what I would be. I would read everything I could lay my hands on. I would establish contact with the literature of other lands, while holding faith with what was worthy in my own country.[22]

MacMahon also evokes the spirit of many other national teachers as they viewed their role as participants in the work of nation-building in the early decades of the new state. They, like he, could not but be aware of a great deal of poverty and social deprivation around them. Yet, they needed to get above this, and help create a new vision. This spirit is caught in the following quotation:

> But adversity also contains at its core the pricking of action. For
> this was also a time of idealism: much of the fervour of the Easter
> Rising persisted into the twenties and thirties; the wave of consu-
> merism and materialism, with its attendant revision of our island
> story, had not yet threatened to engulf us.
>
> We realised that without a vision the people perished. We
> realised that there was nowhere the children could move on the
> social ladder except upwards. Personally, I realised that motiva-
> tion was a first requisite if the lost children of the nation were to
> be cherished. So we set out to establish something bright and shin-
> ing, in which the Irish language would play an important part.[23]

As he faces the heterogeneous group of pupils before him, Mac-
Mahon gives us a marvellous, novelist's listing of the varied
pattern of human nature which they represented:

> So there they were before me, merchants' sons with Little Duke
> shoes, poachers and sons of poachers, weavers of fiction, the
> cunning, the intelligent and the dull. Sometimes the dull were
> cunning in certain respects and the intelligent were dull in others.
> The dutiful, the diligent, the ambitious, the loveable epileptic and
> the equally loveable Down's Syndrome child – all were there; the
> nervous and the fearless, the runaways, the nail-biters, the acci-
> dent-prone, the superficially perfect, and the crossgrained. The
> 'fixers', the precocious, the kickers, the chewers of putty and mor-
> tar, the thumb-suckers, the oats addicts (I had been one myself),
> the sensitive, the nose-bleeders, the mitchers; the finger-fiddlers,
> the gifted, the unpredictable, the ungovernable, the twins indis-
> tinguishable one from the other and who swapped names to avoid
> the consequence of mischief; the prey-seekers, the informers, the
> impenetrable, the esoteric, the horse-lovers, the deaf.[24]

In many of the delightful anecdotes about children in *The Master*, one can recognise the traits he lists in this quotation. One also notes the sense of the human comedy evoked by the list, and the author's embrace and welcome for that variety of personalities involved.

While faced with the mass of his young hopefuls' faces MacMahon never lost sight of the individuality of each of the pupils. Here we note the real educator seeking for the individual traits to nurture and encourage:

> After a time all grew interesting if not precious to me. If I could only plant a seed in the imagination of each one that would fructify later in each unique individual; if only I could find the gift that I sensed was latent in each one of them; perhaps then I would have fulfilled the purpose of my being a teacher. I would receive no thanks – but that did not greatly matter. They need not even know what I had in mind.[25]

As he sought to engage his pupils he realised 'above all I had to identify what would preserve a sense of wonder', a phrase reminiscent of his delightful short-story 'The Windows of Wonder'. As a teacher MacMahon was conscious of the danger in the habituation to years of classroom procedure of pupils' natural curiosity being closed down rather than opened up, and he took steps to prevent it happening.

Many young teachers could learn as much, if not more, from the reflections of a master teacher like MacMahon as from teaching methodology textbooks. In no sense did MacMahon idealise the job as if one was always 'on a high' with pupils. He was well aware of many humdrum and routine aspects of the job. He puts this quite overtly when he states:

All the while I bore in mind that there was nothing highfalutin' about teaching. It often connotes drudgery, conformity, application, monotony, and rota. It can be nerve-sapping in the extreme, but with an unexpected sense of keen self-satisfaction occurring at the oddest moments. I had to achieve a balance. Like many another teacher in the Ireland of that hour I often stopped in mid-class and, looking at the pupils, asked myself, 'Quo vaditis, fratres?' – Where are you to go? Were they to be scattered to the ends of the earth, sinking without trace in a foreign land? Those of affluent parents would inherit a sufficiency of comfort in their own country; the rest were invoiced for Britain or America. To teach them to be survivors, or, to use a modern expression, entrepreneurs, I had to lead, drive or coax them along the harsh road to knowledge.[26]

This sense of reality, of being rooted in the real circumstances of a difficult job, amid harsh socio-economic conditions increases the credibility, the witness of MacMahon to a many-sided occupation.

Among the characteristics of the good teacher, Bryan sets out the following:

Dedication is a prime requisite, as is the gift of infectious enthusiasm. A sense of humour that does not wound is desirable. A clear penetration in the timbre of the teacher's speaking voice is needed: if the voice of the teacher is soporific the words seem to fall to the floor as soon as they are uttered, and the class goes wool-gathering. A love of learning is a most desirable requisite in the good teacher. Versatility of approach to a lesson is important … I mention the importance of the cultivation of a sense of wonder when applied to the minor 'epiphanies of the passing day'… In my deep-rooted opinion the teacher should, above all, act in harmony with the traditions and culture of the school area.[27]

The phrase 'infectious enthusiasm' reminds one of Pearse's attribute of the good teacher 'so infectious an enthusiasm as to foster new enthusiasm'. There is a great deal of wisdom in this designation of teaching qualities, which has the added value of advice having being lived out in practice.

Vocationalism in the Face of Adversity

When one reflects on the professional circumstances in which Bryan MacMahon and his contemporaries exercised their teaching vocation, the question arises as to what sustained their high level of commitment in the face of so many adverse circumstances? From a range of perspectives – training, mode of appointment, curriculum, role of superiors such as managers and inspectors, condition of school buildings, inadequate teaching resources, pupil intake with high levels of socio-economic disadvantage, and salary levels which were parsimonious and downgrading – the conditions in which they operated were anything but propitious. They placed daunting obstacles in the face of maintaining freshness, vigour, commitment and the manifestation of the qualities alluded to in the last quotation.

As was mentioned at the outset of this chapter, few teachers have written reflectively on their experiences of teaching during the decades following political independence. This is to be regretted, but one thinks that Bryan MacMahon was conscious of this when, late in life, he penned *The Master*. It is as if he intended to give voice to that generation. Some years ago I opened a historical exhibition of teaching in the county library in Co. Kerry during an INTO congress. The exhibition was organised by Bryan's former pupil, also a most distinguished teacher, Eamonn Ó Murchú from Listowel. Following my address, Bryan came up to me and stated that he was working on this memoir as he felt that there were important things to put on record. It took a while for *The Master* to be published and I only wish it was as long as I understand the original draft was. Among his other myriad contributions to Irish society, *The Master* is a significant one.

In the opening pages he states:

> I aim to speak for thousands of other teachers, most of them un-sung; ... for thousands of unknown teachers in small substandard schools up and down the country.[28]

This was a noble aim. He was conscious of and valued the tradition in which he worked; but he wished to record for later generations of Irish teachers what it was like to be a school-master in the new state – a state which he loved passionately and whose people he held in high regard. MacMahon writes reflectively and movingly about his generation of teachers as follows:

> Most took up teaching posts in various parts of the country and earned respect, often under difficult conditions. They taught in remote islands and in city slums. They gave unstinted service to the GAA: the spread of national games in the last century came initially from Erin's Hope, the team representing St Patrick's College. Others gave loyal service to organisations such as Comhaltas Ceoltóirí Éireann and Connradh na Gaeilge. As a group they loved Ireland and the things of Ireland and were the pillars of the communities in which they taught.
>
> Some immersed themselves in music, archaeology, or folk-lore. They wrote local guides, and were called on as authorities on local history and genealogy. Some loved learning for its own sake. Lacking comradely stimulus, others took to the bottle, to become eccentrics or alcoholics.[29]

This quiet tone of reflection is a reminder, if one were needed, of the contribution of that generation of teachers to the way of life in the new state. What is surprising is not that a small minority ran into difficulties, but that so many achieved so much in the face of adversity. What sustained them? It would seem that the *dúchas*, the *cultúr*, the tradition from which they came, coupled with personal talent, a love of learning and a sense of patriotism towards the new state were what carried them through. They were a bridging generation between the old and the new, and bequeathed much of value to Irish society and to later generations of teachers. They passed on the torch of learning and helped to preserve that 'golden thread' of continuity of valuing the role of the teacher which is so deeply rooted in Irish educational history and tradition.

1 John Coolahan, 'The Education Bill of 1919 – Problems of Educational Reform', *Proceedings of the Educational Studies Association of Ireland* (Galway: Galway University Press, 1979), pp. 11–31.

2 Reported in *The Irish School Weekly*, 11 February 1922, p. 127.

3 *National Programme of Primary Instruction Issued by the National Programme Conference* (Dublin: Educational Company, 1922).

4 *Report and Programme Presented by the National Programme Conference* (Dublin: Stationery Office, 1926).

5 *Dáil Debates*, vol. li (11/4/34), col. 1603.

6 *Revised Programme of Primary Instruction* (Dublin: Stationery Office, 1934).

7 John Coolahan, 'Education in the Training Colleges, 1877–1977', *Two Centenary Lectures* (Dublin: Our Lady of Mercy College, 1977).

8 Bryan MacMahon, *The Master* (Dublin: Poolbeg Press, 1992), p. 4.

9 Quoted in *The Times Educational Supplement*, 29 October 1921, p. 323.

10 MacMahon, *The Master*.

11 *Circular to Inspectors* (Aireacht An Oideachais), February 1924, p. 4.

12 Dáil Debate on Education Estimates, June 1940.

13 MacMahon, *The Master*, p. 114.

14 *Ibid.*, p. 115.

15 T. J. O'Connell, *History of the Irish National Teachers' Organisation, 1868–1968* (Dublin: INTO, 1969; and INTO Archives).

16 MacMahon, *The Master*, p. 24.

17 *Ibid.*, pp. 9, 10.

18 *Ibid.*, p. 12.

19 *Ibid.*, p. 30.

20 *Ibid.*, p. 31.

21 *Ibid.*, p. 20.

22 *Ibid.*, p. 8.

23 *Ibid.*, p. 8.

24 *Ibid.*, p. 18.

25 *Ibid.*, p. 18.

26 *Ibid.*, p. 23.

27 *Ibid.*, pp. 105, 106.

28 *Ibid.*, p. 8.

29 *Ibid.*, p. 8.